the common base of social work practice

Other Books by Harriett M. Bartlett

Medical Social Work: A Study of Current Aims and Methods in Medical Social Case Work. Chicago: American Association of Medical Social Workers, 1934.

The Participation of Medical Social Workers in the Teaching of Medical Students. Chicago: American Association of Medical Social Workers, 1939.

Some Aspects of Social Casework in a Medical Setting: A Study in the Field of Medical Social Work. Chicago: American Association of Medical Social Workers, 1940.

50 Years of Social Work in the Medical Setting: Past Significance/Future Outlook. New York: National Association of Social Workers, 1957.

Analyzing Social Work Practice by Fields. New York: National Association of Social Workers, 1961.

Social Work Practice in the Health Field. New York: National Association of Social Workers, 1961.

the common base of social work practice

HARRIETT M. BARTLETT

with the assistance of

BEATRICE N. SAUNDERS

NATIONAL ASSOCIATION OF SOCIAL WORKERS INC.
2 PARK AVENUE, NEW YORK, N.Y. 10016

Price: $4.00

contents

acknowledgments

This monograph, which was conceived in 1965, has its roots in the NASW projects concerned with social work practice and carries on the stream of thinking about practice. The discussion of professional problems in those projects has been an important source of ideas. The following persons, all of whom read more than one draft, acted as consultants on this monograph: Bess S. Dana, Alice Taylor Davis, William E. Gordon, Margaret L. Schutz, and Theodate H. Soule. As the writing progressed through its various stages, the consultants contributed many significant questions and suggestions that have greatly clarified and enriched the material. Most of the practice questions here considered have been discussed over the years with William Gordon and Margaret Schutz; thus our shared thinking has influenced this material throughout. I am indebted also to other professional associates who conferred with me on sections of the monograph or provided material regarding trends and issues in social work practice. Special thanks are given to Walter L. Kindelsperger and Jeanette Regensburg, who read the first draft and offered their thoughtful comments.

I wish to express deep appreciation to Beatrice Saunders for her editorial assistance in the preparation of the monograph. The problem of achieving basic thinking in a period of accelerating change and uncertainty, both in the profession and in society, has been so difficult as at times to seem almost insoluble. As we worked together over the successive drafts, Mrs. Saunders helped me toward expressing the essential ideas and presenting them in a form and order best suited to the subject, the audience, and the times. Without her discerning assistance and steady support this monograph could not have come to fruition. Wendy Almeleh gave valuable assistance in the final stages of preparing the manuscript for publication. Finally, I wish to express appreciation for the work of Jessie B. MacDonald, who bore the main responsibility for typing the manuscripts.

Having completed an analysis of this kind, in which the ideas have been slowly developed and constantly reworked over a considerable period, the writer feels at last ready to start writing the whole monograph again from the beginning. Since this is not possible, it must be sent forth as it is, with deep appreciation to all who have given help.

introduction

One of the strongest forces determining the growth of a profession is the way in which the members themselves perceive and define what they are doing or trying to do—their goals, knowledge, and techniques. At this moment in history, social work has the potential for making an important and distinctive contribution to society. Forward movement and growth depend on the interest and capacity of social workers to identify and clarify the essential strengths and limitations of their profession and to consolidate the strengths to provide a powerful source of action.

In the midst of enormous pressures from a changing society that call for broad, flexible, and rapid responses, some social workers have despaired that their profession can meet the demand. They feel that efforts to strengthen the profession itself will be too slow and inadequate. Others reject efforts to strengthen the profession for other reasons, for example, because they perceive such action as inevitably leading to "professionalism" in the sense of narrowness, rigidity, insensitivity, and bureaucracy. This failure of confidence in the profession results partly from the lack of a clear perception of social work for, without a solid and convincing image of the profession, social workers can hardly grasp its strength.

We have chosen to focus directly on the social work profession as having attained a key position in the multiple welfare activities of our society. This position carries a responsibility for leadership and action, which in turn demands full use of the profession's

9

powers. Today social work possesses many unrecognized strengths but it must also face and deal with its limitations. In our judgment the necessary steps can be taken without leading to narrow professionalism. The important point is to take a broad look at social work and the identification of its potential.

This monograph is about social work practice. It is not a description of practice or an analysis of practice but rather a consideration of social workers' *ways of thinking* about their practice. In the interests of consistency, the practice viewpoint is maintained throughout; no attempt is made to consider educational implications or other professional aspects.

Nor is this a formal research study. The method is that of analysis and description based upon the writer's experience in social work practice and education, including continuous participation in the programs of professional organizations over an extended period. A special effort is made to identify trends in social work thinking and, when dysjunctions are found, to extend the conceptualization to make connections between ideas. Important steps in social work thinking will be examined in a search for creative ideas, latent influences and barriers, and long-term developments. The coverage is intended to be comprehensive but not exhaustive of all possible approaches.

In recent decades, social work has made marked advances through bringing its members together in nationwide organizations. Vigorous thinking has been going on in various separate facets of its practice. Significant progress has also been made in bringing order into the thinking about overall practice; but such thinking is difficult and tends to lag. The purpose of this monograph is to carry on the stream of broad thinking about practice, viewed as the practice of the whole profession. The effort here is to bring together some of the pertinent ideas and questions so that they can be viewed in relation to each other, not to formulate one single system of concepts and theory. The emphasis is on continuity and the convergence of ideas. Hopefully this endeavor will put some of the pieces together, make them more visible and orderly, stimulate others to work on the various problems involved, and, finally, generate ongoing thinking in the same or new directions.

part one

backgrounds

1

seeking the
strengths of
social work

"What are people for?" asks Julian Huxley. "To achieve a higher quality of life," is his answer.[1] Human cultural evolution, he says, operates through a process of challenge and response. Something in the existing situation acts as a stimulus or challenge to human society or mind, and human society and mind make some sort of response. It may not always be the right response, but there is always a process resulting in directed change.[2]

This kind of challenge and response is evident in our society today in relation to a growing number of acute social problems, such as the urban crisis, civil rights, poverty, and delinquency. Efforts to deal with these problems are, as Huxley indicates, sometimes poorly directed, so that results do not produce the desired improvement in human welfare and may even create new problems.

Many social workers have felt strongly that they should be able

---

[1] *The Human Crisis* (Seattle: University of Washington Press, 1963), p. 27.

[2] *Ibid.*, p. 22.

to make a significant contribution to the alleviation or solution of these large social problems in addition to rendering their traditional services to individuals, groups, and communities. In fact, social workers are already involved in such extended efforts but their impact has not been in proportion to their hope. Actually, there is reason to believe that what social work has to give is particularly relevant to society's needs today, but clear thinking on such matters is difficult in the face of the confusions, uncertainties, and fears that beset all mankind. In spite of the threat of social disorganization, the unexampled plasticity of human affairs currently offers an enlarged scope for good that appears only rarely in history.[3]

In the 1960s, after more than fifty years of growth, the social work profession faced a period of social change that presented problems and opportunities of an unprecedented nature. Immediate and forceful responses were required but social workers found themselves unready to act quickly. Although repeated analysis has shown that social work has many of the attributes of a profession (as will be discussed later), its strengths are still not fully recognized or developed. Because of this lack of recognition, the contribution its members are making in society is less effective than it might be. How, then, can these strengths be more fully put to use?

A short time before this period of rapid social change, as part of a professional program for the study of practice, an approach for analyzing fields of practice in social work was developed and applied in one field.[4] This approach involved three steps: (1) it started from the essential elements in social work as a base, (2) it moved to an assessment of the field in which social work practice was to take place, and then (3) it applied the essential elements in the field to identify the characteristics of the resulting practice. Considerable evidence was received that this approach was useful to many social workers in this country and abroad for viewing and analyzing their practice comprehensively. Soon there-

---

[3] *See* William H. McNeill, *The Rise of the West* (Chicago: University of Chicago Press, 1963), p. 807.

[4] Harriett M. Bartlett, *Analyzing Social Work Practice by Fields* and *Social Work Practice in the Health Field* (New York: National Association of Social Workers, 1961).

after the urgent need to re-examine social workers' activities because of the remarkable changes taking place in American society suggested that the approach for analyzing fields might now be relevant and illuminating for an analysis of all social work practice.

In accordance with that approach, the hypothesis of this discussion is that social work, having developed so far, can make its greatest contribution in society by developing even further as a strong profession. After half a century of exploring various forms of service, social workers are now able for the first time to perceive clearly the wide scope of their potential service. After prolonged concentration on work with individuals and small groups, the profession has been roughly jolted by the sudden recognition of urgent social problems and the emergence of proliferating health and social welfare programs. In exploring anew their contribution to poverty, delinquency, urban development, and similar social problems, social workers can no longer work within the confines of their own agencies and at their own pace but must be ready to work through new channels and often in collaboration with new types of associates, such as engineers, city planners, political scientists, public administration experts, and indigenous neighborhood workers. Innovation is in the air and flexibility is a prerequisite.

Probably the chief characteristic of this change is the radical broadening of social work practice in both viewpoint and actuality. The range of people to be served, programs in which to operate, and associates with whom to collaborate has suddenly opened out like a fan. The older criteria for teamwork and client service no longer apply in the same way. Large numbers of social workers are moving into the new areas of practice with interest and enthusiasm, which is desirable. With the current emphasis on modifying social conditions and social programs, there is, however, a tendency to reject social work's earlier concern with individuals and small groups as inadequate in today's society. Such differences could lead to an increasing and eventually sharp separation between two views of social work practice. Under such circumstances the strength of the profession would be undermined and its unity threatened. *Thus a major decision before the profession is whether it intends to make its expressed interest in individuals, groups, and communities real and effective and how it will bring this about.*

While social work is generally regarded as having attained professional status, it cannot be regarded yet as a strong profession. In a partly formed, maturing profession such as this, operating in a still relatively undefined area, vigorous effort is needed to strengthen the growth process, particularly in a time of rapid social change, conflicting forces, and accelerating need. What is involved might be called "profession-building." In today's world, such growth is not likely to take place naturally through the relatively uncoordinated efforts of thousands of social workers. It is true that social workers are noted for their proclivity for self-examination and self-criticism, but they have tended too much to stop with raising questions. What is needed is the kind of deliberate action undertaken by a scientist, who defines a problem, develops one or more hypotheses to meet it, and moves steadily ahead over a period of years to test the hypotheses and seek the necessary solutions. In social work this means conscious movement toward positive intellectual solutions of the problems confronting the profession.

Deliberate effort to identify the central questions relating to practice, as well as more planning about effective deployment of the profession's resources, is needed. The experience of the first Commission on Practice of the National Association of Social Workers, which undertook pioneer work in 1955, suggests the strategic value of developing channels and expectations for such integrated and cumulative thinking. The strong program of the Council on Social Work Education is also essential. But wider recognition throughout the whole profession and more creative thinking from larger numbers of members are needed to solve the truly complex problems of social work practice. *How to engage itself to deal effectively with its great but unrealized potential is perhaps the most important single decision before the profession at this time.*

Steps in Thinking Before the Profession

In view of the urgent decisions confronting the profession regarding its own practice, we can now identify certain steps in thinking that lie ahead, in moving toward realization of the profession's potential. These may be stated in the following propositions:

■ *It is important to be able to view the entirety of social work practice.* Convergence will not be obtained if practitioners, teachers, administrators, and research workers all operate with different perspectives and within differing frames of reference. In recent years writers in *Science,* the journal of the American Association for the Advancement of Science, have been pointing out that we are in the midst of a strong trend toward breaking down phenomena and experience into smaller and smaller entities, but that many of the answers to today's problems will be found only through concepts and hypotheses that promote synthesis.[5] Such integrative thinking is needed in social work today.

■ *Identification of social work's particular focus—its area of central concern as a profession—comes as a first specific, logical step.* A balance must be found between the overambitious attempt to meet all of society's demands and the narrow involvement in limited techniques. When eventually defined, the central focus will appear as a single concept or constellation of concepts on which practice can be based and around which theory can be developed.

■ *The common elements in social work need to be identified and established as the base for all social work practice.* The various segments of practice, still too fragmented, need to be brought together. Here will fall the fields and other areas of practice concerned with particular groups or problems, as well as the methods and interventive approaches. Social workers have always identified most easily with "fields" or with "methods." The persistent unsolved problem is still to be dealt with, namely, what is common and what is different in these various types of practice? And how can the likenesses and the differences be most effectively related to each other to produce an integrated social work practice? This step in thinking could not and cannot be reached until social

---

[5] *See,* for example, Emmanuel G. Mesthene, "Our Threatened Planet: The Technological Plague," review of Barry Commoner, *Science and Survival* (New York: Viking Press, 1966), in *Science,* Vol. 155, No. 3761 (January 27, 1967), pp. 441–442; David B. Truman, "The Social Sciences and Public Policy," *Science,* Vol. 160, No. 3827 (May 3, 1968), pp. 508–512; and Don K. Price, "Purists and Politicians," *Science,* Vol. 163, No. 3862 (January 3, 1969), pp. 25–31.

workers have made sufficient progress in identifying the social work focus and common base of practice to allow for the required processes of analysis and synthesis.

  ■ *Social work needs to recognize, examine, and deal with the limitations and dilemmas in its own thinking.* Social work writers point out the existence of latent and implicit modes of thinking that have been producing the lags, inconsistencies, and contradictions described.[6] Social work is becoming aware of the need to understand its peculiar characteristics as a growing profession in both their positive and negative implications.

  ■ *Failure in knowledge-building is being recognized as the largest problem and most important area of undeveloped potential.* Extremely complex but also stimulating and challenging questions arise as to the necessary steps in focusing, formulating, systematizing, and testing social work knowledge. Here, especially, organized ways for social workers to get together to work on such problems are essential—the NASW Commission on Practice is a case in point.

  ■ *Since the purpose of all these steps is to produce leaders and practitioners competent to make the needed contribution to society, there must be ongoing thinking about how the essential elements of such practice can be identified by and incorporated in the members of this profession.* Here practice and education work together. It is an assumption of this monograph that social work will be strengthened when the practice elements are more clearly defined and tested than has been customary in the past. Furthermore, such clarification and testing within the overall professional frame of reference should go hand in hand with their translation into educational terms for the curriculum, the analysis of practice and the building of curriculum being two phases of the same process.

Concept of a Profession

Of importance in this monograph is the general concept of a profession as developed in Western society and particularly in this

---

  [6] *See,* for example, Alfred J. Kahn, "The Nature of Social Work Knowledge," in Cora Kasius, ed., *New Directions in Social Work* (New York: Harper & Bros., 1954), pp. 194–214; Alfred Kadushin, "The Knowledge

country.[7] Authorities usually emphasize two essential attributes: (1) a high degree of generalized and systematic knowledge and (2) orientation to the community interest rather than to individual self-interest.[8] The profession's knowledge and values, along with special techniques based upon them, are transmissible through education. Professions are responsible for standards of practice and the competence of their members. Professional practice, by its very nature, involves a large amount of discretion. It has been further pointed out that practice which involves direct and personal relating to clients, along with considerable exercise of personal judgment, evokes a special feeling of responsibility.

The major distinction between a profession and an occupation is usually regarded as being the substantial body of knowledge on which a profession rests. One type of occupation, sometimes described as a "semiprofession," makes use of technical skills and establishes as its knowledge base a body of experience derived from occupational practice. Nursing and social work, as now practiced, could be so described.[9] Some social workers think that social work should remain an occupation. This opinion is in opposition to the one which considers that social work should move in the direction of developing as a profession.

Base of Social Work," in Alfred J. Kahn, ed., *Issues in American Social Work* (New York: Columbia University Press, 1959), pp. 39–79.

[7] *See* A. M. Carr-Saunders and P. A. Wilson, *The Professions* (Oxford, England: Clarendon Press, 1933); Abraham Flexner, "Is Social Work a Profession?" in *Proceedings of the National Conference of Charities and Correction* (Chicago: National Conference of Charities and Correction, 1915), pp. 576–590; Ernest Greenwood, "Attributes of a Profession," *Social Work*, Vol. 2. No. 3 (July 1957), pp. 45–55; Ralph W. Tyler, "Distinctive Attributes of Education for the Professions," *Social Work Journal*, Vol. 33, No. 2 (April 1952), pp. 55–57; and "The Professions," *Daedalus*, Vol. 92, No. 4 (Fall 1963), whole issue.

[8] Bernard Barber, "Some Problems in the Sociology of the Professions," *Daedalus*, Vol. 92, No. 4 (Fall 1963), p. 672.

[9] Henry J. Meyer, "Professionalization and Social Work," in Kahn, ed., *op. cit.*, pp. 323–324; and A. M. Carr-Saunders, "Metropolitan Conditions and Traditional Professional Relationships," in R. M. Fisher, ed., *The Metropolis in Modern Life* (New York: Doubleday & Co., 1955), pp. 280–281, as summarized by A. J. Reiss, Jr., "Occupational Mobility of Professional Workers," *American Sociological Review*, Vol. 20, No. 6 (December 1955), p. 693.

Two core functions of professions are professional practice and professional education. In addition, professions have many other important functions, such as the organization of their members to facilitate the accomplishment of the objectives, formulation of a code of ethics, recruitment of personnel, public relations, maintenance of co-operative relationships with institutions and other personnel engaged in their general area of service, and meeting the interests of their own members.

In examining practice, questions must be asked about how far and in what way social workers are recognizing the common elements in their practice, moving toward integrative thinking about them, and making the strengths of their profession increasingly effective in society. Before this period of social change, forces were already at work within the profession to consolidate its strengths. These appeared particularly in the form of movement toward a "generic" curriculum in schools of social work and the organization of national professional associations. In practice itself, however, progress was slower. In trying to understand why this should be so we shall begin by examining and tracing some early influences and trends that shaped social workers' perceptions of their professional practice.[10]

---

[10] After this monograph went to press in late 1969, the National Association of Social Workers took action through a referendum to broaden its *regular* membership by adding the following: BA degree holders who have completed an undergraduate program in social work that meets criteria established by the Council on Social Work Education, students enrolled in accredited graduate schools of social work, and certain persons holding doctoral degrees in related fields. A category of *associate membership* was established to include bachelor's degree holders from any field who are currently employed in a social work capacity. Responsibility for establishing additional criteria was placed with the NASW Board of Directors. *See* "Referendum: Amendments to Bylaws," and "The Ballots in Brief: What You Are Asked To Vote On," *NASW News*, Vol. 15, No. 1 (November 1969), p. 2. In the author's opinion, the need to recognize and develop the strengths of social work, as discussed in this monograph, is not only relevant to the situation created by the NASW action, but becomes even more urgent than before because of the increased scope and complexity of the practice.

2

early trends

Early social work was characterized by two types of effort—
social reform and assistance to individuals and families under
stress. Encompassed under social reform were a variety of community efforts revealing a strong sense of responsibility for improving the welfare of those who were deprived or handicapped.
Social workers perceived their role as that of calling attention to
the problem, rousing the public conscience, speaking for the people involved and stimulating their participation, offering evidence
as to the nature of their needs, and advocating appropriate preventive or corrective measures. Their actions were directed toward
eliminating or alleviating social problems and conditions affecting
whole communities or population groups, as for instance in relation to child welfare or the employment of women. Social work
leadership made a significant impact on social policy through the
improvement of public welfare services and enlargement of programs of voluntary social agencies. Another approach was
through the settlements, which emphasized being close to people,
living and working among them in the neighborhood, offering
opportunities to grow toward self-direction and fuller participation
as citizens in a democratic society, and advocating social measures
to improve living conditions.

The other major phase of social work practice—assistance to
individuals and families under stress—developed out of the charity
organization movement. This work was first performed by volun-

21

teers, but by the turn of the century it was recognized that persons who were to give individualized services in relation to the complex problems of poverty and family life required training. Shortly before and after 1900, the first schools of social work were established and professional workers took the place of friendly visitors. Out of this early practice and these schools developed the concept of social work as a skilled process of giving help.

While social work practitioners soon regarded themselves as professional workers, the forces operating in this formative period encouraged differences rather than integration. During the first half century of social work history, an observer viewing the practice widely would have seen a profession growing through its separate parts. The concepts so developed were sufficiently related to hold social workers together and, for a considerable period, this pattern of practice, in spite of its lack of integration, continued to stimulate the growth of the profession.

Social Work Practice in Separate Fields

An early and important segment of practice was known as the "field of practice." In our modern industrial civilization, societies establish social institutions to provide services required to meet the various basic human needs, such as family maintenance, shelter, education, and health or to deal with societal problems such as delinquency. Since there are always some people whose needs are not met by the services and since the manner in which services are rendered may block effective use by those who need them, social workers were drawn into practice in one field after another. By the time social work practice began to develop visibility in the twenties and thirties, it was growing rapidly in the separate fields. There was at that time no concept of professional social work practice as a single entity.

By the end of the twenties, five fields of practice had emerged —family and child welfare, in which social workers were employed in social welfare agencies, and medical, psychiatric, and school social work, in which social workers were employed in non-social work agencies.[1] Social workers in these fields worked intensively,

---

[1] The American Association of Social Workers, established in 1921, was an overall organization representing social work as a whole. Its program

but within their own field, to clarify the nature of their competence. Medical social workers had a continuing committee for analysis of practice from 1922 on and psychiatric social workers established such a committee later.   What intellectual tools were then available for the analysis of practice?   What approaches were used?

Two concepts were predominant at that time, the concept of *social work method* and the concept of *setting*. The concept of method developed first around casework and later in relation to group work and community organization.   It rested on selected clusters of theory concerning human behavior.   The concept of setting referred to the organizational environment within which the service was given.   This concept directed attention to the characteristics of the agencies and programs in which social work had to find a place.   The social structure of the hospital and public school, the goals and methods of physicians and teachers, the nature of the client group, and similar factors were analyzed and described.   This approach tended to emphasize what was different among the fields and thus, while it stimulated thinking about the social work contribution and clarified practice within the fields, it tended to produce greater fragmentation in practice as a whole.

Social workers defined their central problem and responsibility as that characteristic of the particular field.   In child welfare, the social worker's central responsibility was defined as meeting the needs of the child when parental responsibility broke down and communities failed to provide the resources and protection required by children and families.   For a considerable period this responsibility was viewed primarily as providing substitute care, particularly in the form of foster home care for the child. As time went on, however, there was increasing emphasis on supporting and strengthening the family by providing services in the home.[2]

Family welfare, in addition to its contribution to casework

---

emphasized personnel standards and social action and gave relatively less attention to leadership or co-ordination of effort in the development of professional thinking about practice.

[2] *Child Welfare as a Field of Social Work Practice* (New York: Child Welfare League of America, 1959).

thinking, was also keeping the concept of the family before social work practitioners. All social workers are concerned with families but, by the nature of their work, family workers have always had this as their primary concern. After the social security program no longer made it as necessary for family agencies to be primarily concerned with financial problems, interest moved toward psychosocial problems, such as marital difficulties. In the fifties, an outburst of interest in family diagnosis and treatment in a number of professions stimulated family workers to extend their interest in this direction.[3]

In the medical setting social workers found a sharp distinction between the frames of reference of the dominant profession, medicine, and the growing perspective of social work. The problem was, therefore, not only to find a place in the setting but also to find a way of bringing these two perspectives together. How could scientific knowledge regarding disease and methods of medical care be related more sensitively to the needs of the patient as a person? [4]

In school social work the primary focus was on the child's difficulties in relation to and use of the school and the educational program. In this field there was not a large visible body of knowledge about the central problem—in this instance, the nature of learning and the educational process—as there was in some other fields. The emphasis was, therefore, on understanding and working with the school as an institution, on the one hand, and with the child and his family, on the other.[5]

In mental health the frames of reference of the major professional group (psychiatry) and of social work were closer than in any of the other fields involving multidisciplinary practice. Diagnosis was customarily carried out in interdisciplinary conferences and the psychiatric diagnosis was immediately relevant for the social worker's understanding of the patient and his needs. For these reasons, social work thinking, as expressed in its litera-

---

[3] See "Family Casework in the Interest of Children," Social Casework, Vol. 39, Nos. 2–3 (February–March 1958), whole issue.

[4] Harriett M. Bartlett, Some Aspects of Social Casework in a Medical Setting (Chicago: American Association of Medical Social Workers, 1940).

[5] Mildred Sikkema, School Social Work Practice in Twelve Communities (New York: American Association of Social Workers, 1953).

ture and teaching, emphasized the psychic aspects of the problem and the process of giving help through direct professional relationship with the individual. This was a major contribution to social casework and social work understanding of human behavior but was heavily weighted on one side of the person-environment complex with which social workers are concerned.[6]

Turning now from these earlier fields of practice: in the forties the development of two method-oriented fields—group work and community organization—extended social work practice in new directions. These were concerned not only with services to groups and communities but also with methods related specifically to the rendering of these services. By the midcentury these two fields were still in the stage of defining their focus and concepts.[7]

Social work in corrections did not gain recognition as a field until later than the others. In the fifties, through the support of the U.S. Children's Bureau and the Council on Social Work Education, rapid progress was made in defining social work practice in corrections. Coming as it did at a later stage in the profession's development, social work in corrections did not have to go through some of the growing pains of the older fields. A particular contribution was made from this field to the understanding of problems of authority, as faced by both clients and social workers.[8]

Social work in public welfare (or public assistance) has been at times described as a field of practice, but it did not become separately organized within the structure of the profession. Because of its concern with families and children, this area of practice was most frequently included within the fields of family and child welfare.

During the early period of working in various fields, up to the

---

[6] Tessie D. Berkman, *Practice of Social Workers in Psychiatric Hospitals and Clinics* (New York: American Association of Psychiatric Social Workers, 1953).

[7] Gertrude Wilson and Gladys Ryland, *Social Group Work Practice* (Cambridge, Mass.: Riverside Press, 1949); and *Community Organization: Its Nature and Setting* (New York: American Association of Social Workers, 1947).

[8] Elliot Studt, *Education for Social Workers in the Correctional Field* (New York: Council on Social Work Education, 1959).

fifties, social workers were learning about a wide range of social problems. They learned how the problems affected individuals and families and how the people themselves felt about the difficulties. Social workers also acquired valuable experience in collaborating with other personnel, particularly members of other professions, and in making contributions to the agencies and programs in which they worked. The problems were viewed as characteristic of particular areas of practice, such as public welfare or mental health. The ways of working with other personnel and contributing to agency programs were considered to be associated with particular settings. These ideas about practice were discussed in the literature and in teaching but, for reasons to be considered later, were not presented as concepts or knowledge belonging to all social work and capable of leading toward an integrated view of its practice.

Thus practice in the fields was moving social work toward professional development but in an unco-ordinated manner. The emphasis on the differences among the settings within which social workers practiced continued to be a divisive factor. In a move to offset this, Perlman pointed out in 1949 that features claimed by practitioners as characteristic of one or another setting, such as teamwork with other professions, were actually relevant for all the settings. She thus emphasized the generic aspects of settings.[9] This was a helpful integrative idea but was not strong enough to overcome the fragmentation because of limitations inherent in the concept of setting itself. What was not perceived by the practitioners of that period was that this concept rested on factors *outside* their practice—elements in the agency or program—which, it is true, molded their work in important ways but were external to it. What social work particularly needed was a conceptual approach based on the essential elements *within* its own practice, no matter where the worker practiced.

Agency and Profession

The practice of social work is characteristically carried on in and through health and welfare agencies and programs. The so-

---

[9] Helen Harris Perlman, "Generic Aspects of Specific Casework Settings," *Social Service Review,* Vol. 23, No. 3 (September 1949), pp. 293–301.

cial worker has been an employed person operating in specific agencies. Up to this time there has been no "general practice," in the sense in which it is found in some professions, although recently a growing private practice has developed, the focus of which is not yet clearly defined.

Like fields of practice, agencies have exerted an important influence on the development of social work practice and the growth of the profession. Agencies and programs are socially and legally established structures for organizing, administering, and delivering services and bringing resources to the people who need and want them. Social work may be one of the professional services so offered and, in a welfare agency, may be the major service. Under these circumstances a professional social worker renders the core service and the social work profession primarily determines and develops the necessary competence.

The support that the agency board and administration give to social work is of major importance in relation to the contribution the profession can make in society. When administered by social workers, social agencies have continually given leadership in extending services in the community and identifying new needs requiring additional services. The collaboration between agencies and schools in developing social work education has been an outstanding feature of this profession from earliest times.

In our society employment of professional personnel by agencies and programs is increasing and independent practice is decreasing.[10] One reason for this is the growth of specialization, with a consequent increase in multidisciplinary practice. In working primarily in agencies, social workers are thus in line with a general social trend. Several large issues are involved in such professional practice within agency programs. The employed practitioner must be able to relate to the agency in such a way as to further its purposes but at the same time to retain his own identity. There is always tension between these two requirements.[11] Sociological theory and organizational theory are rapidly

---

[10] Eliot Freidson, "The Organization of Medical Practice," in Howard E. Freeman, Sol Levine, and Leo G. Reeder, eds., *Handbook of Medical Sociology* (Englewood Cliffs, N. J.: Prentice-Hall, 1963), pp. 302–303.

[11] Harriett M. Bartlett, *Social Work Practice in the Health Field* (New York: National Association of Social Workers, 1961), pp. 47–60.

building up knowledge regarding the nature of structure and behavior in modern complex organizations. Vinter has discussed these issues in a clarifying manner as they appear in social work practice. He shows that, from the viewpoint of the profession, the agency as a bureaucratic structure may not allow the practitioners sufficient freedom for their essential operations. From the viewpoint of the agency, on the other hand, the freedom demanded by professionals may confuse and block the fulfillment of its goals.[12] Without doubt, this aspect of the agency-profession relationship requires further study.

Blurring of Practice Concepts

The tendency to perceive and discuss social work practice in terms of agency practice has been strong all through the history of social work. In the early days the agencies were the most conspicuous feature of the social welfare field. Social work practice was as yet hardly visible as an entity. It was the agencies that were chartered by the community and thus it was through the agencies that social workers found their beginning security and identity.

The concepts of social welfare, social agency, and social work have been continuously blurred. Textbooks on social work discuss agency programs and professional practice interchangeably. Articles in social work journals not infrequently bear titles suggesting social work practice but offer content related to agency services. During the first fifty years, social work research dealt largely with agency organization, structure, and services, including such operations as recording and statistics. It was not until the midcentury, when social workers became fully aware of their own profession and began to develop a comprehensive perception of their practice, that they recognized their own contribution as a potential force in society.

The problem of making the necessary distinction appears most clearly in the family and child welfare fields. In American society there has been less initiative in establishing welfare agencies

---

[12] Robert D. Vinter, "The Social Structure of Service," in Alfred J. Kahn, ed., *Issues in American Social Work* (New York: Columbia University Press, 1959), pp. 242–269; and Vinter, "Analysis of Treatment Organizations," *Social Work*, Vol. 8, No. 3 (July 1963), pp. 3–15.

than in establishing health, educational, and correctional agencies. There was no social security program and welfare as a governmental responsibility was barely visualized. Voluntary welfare agencies were therefore established to meet the needs. In family and child welfare, national organizations composed of member agencies assumed leadership for developing goals and standards of practice for both agency programs and the practice of social workers employed in the agencies.[13] Since it seemed clear at that time that all these activities could be regarded as social work, it did not seem necessary to make any distinction between agency and profession.

Meanwhile, other social workers were practicing in hospitals and schools, where they worked in association with other professions in non-social work settings. Since they could not form associations on an agency base, they formed professional associations composed of individual practitioners. Furthermore, because they had to answer the question of what they were bringing that was new and would represent an addition to the program they were entering, they were forced from the beginning to concentrate attention on their own professional practice in order to evaluate and demonstrate its contribution to the overall agency.

In family and child welfare, although casework was clearly visualized as a professional process, it continued to be tied to the agency, as can be seen in the persistent phrase "casework agency." In child welfare, services had always been rendered through a variety of other personnel and resources, such as foster homes, adoptive homes, and children's institutions. Family welfare also, as time went on, included such services as those of homemakers. Many of these services were a part of the agency program and were supervised by the social work staff, so that the line between agency and professional social work practice was not clear.

Articles in the *Social Work Year Book* (issued every three years starting in 1929) describing the different fields reveal the trends in thinking about profession and agency. In the early

---

[13] In 1911 the family agencies formed a federation—the National Association of Societies for Organizing Charity—that was a forerunner of the present Family Service Association of America. In 1920 the Child Welfare League of America was founded.

period, the articles on medical and psychiatric social work focused on the practice of the social worker, while those on family and child welfare focused on the agency and its program. In the first volume of the *Encyclopedia of Social Work* (which followed the year book in 1965), there is for the first time a discussion of "professional aspects" in the article on child welfare, but the article on family social work continues to be written from the viewpoint of agency services. School social work falls between these two approaches, starting with an emphasis on the agency, but always with some mention of social work practitioners, and moving toward a focus on social work practice. The field of correctional services, which developed slowly, was variously described in the *Social Work Year Book* in agency terms, until an article clearly focused on social work practice in corrections appeared in the 1965 *Encyclopedia of Social Work*.[14]

The early failure to distinguish between social welfare and social work added to the confusion. The formation of the Council on Social Work Education and the National Association of Social Workers in the fifties increased the visibility of the social work profession. At that time, the National Conference of Social Work changed its name to the National Conference on Social Welfare in recognition that its scope was broader than social work.

Distinguishing Agency and Profession

At the level of individual practice, social workers are guided in many appropriate ways by the programs and policies of their employing agencies. They are not, however, stimulated to examine the contribution of their profession until they can perceive the profession clearly as an independent social institution that has responsibility to define its own goals, content, and standards. In the author's opinion, failure to make the distinction between agency and profession has been one important obstacle to the clarification of professional practice.

---

[14] *See* Zitha R. Turitz and Rebecca Smith, "Child Welfare," pp. 137–145; Clark W. Blackburn, "Family Social Work," pp. 309–319; and Elliot Studt, "Correctional Services (Social Work Practice in)," pp. 219–225, *Encyclopedia of Social Work* (New York: National Association of Social Workers, 1965).

As the movement toward unification of the social work profession has proceeded, many social workers have become aware that the profession possesses strengths that are lacking in agencies. Agencies are restricted in relation to program planning and delivery of service because of their separateness and inflexibility. In spite of years of effort through community councils, progress toward co-ordination of agency programs has been limited and not in line with early hopes and expectations. Agencies too often have been resistant to change. Gaps in the community's services have persisted and even seemed to increase in spite of persistent effort to expand agency services when needed.

The social work profession has a nationwide scope. It has, on the one hand, greater continuity and consistency and, on the other hand, greater flexibility than is found in a group of community agencies. Thus there is the possibility that the profession may in the long run have greater impact on social need and social change than the agencies.

One of the problems to which we will return is the question of how the social worker can be aware of and be most effective in making the essential contribution to his profession, whether he is operating in a traditional agency or in some other capacity in today's emerging programs. In spite of steady clarification, confusion about agencies and social work practice continues.[15] In discussing and writing about social work, social workers continue to move from agency to professional practice and back again, without recognizing the differences between them or identifying the characteristics and responsibilities of each. Together the profession and the agencies should be able to offer a flexible and adequate response to society's needs, but this requires that social workers recognize their own functions and responsibilities as related to, but also distinguished from, those of the agencies.

A Practice Model Based on Method and Skill

Practice in separate fields and practice in agencies were among the earliest influences shaping the growth of the profession. Even

---

[15] Alan D. Wade, "The Social Worker in the Political Process," *The Social Welfare Forum, 1966* (New York: Columbia University Press, 1966), pp. 58–59.

more important, but developing at a somewhat slower pace, were social workers' own perceptions regarding the professional nature of their practice and the manner in which they defined these perceptions.

The first directions that proved useful for building professional practice developed from the two original types of social work—social reform and family service. Work with groups and community problems was developing as a social work activity in the twenties and thirties but did not attain professional formulation until later. An interesting question is why social science concepts concerning social relationships were not of more influence in early social work. At that time, sociologists like Simmel and Cooley were already presenting a forceful body of theory on social process, communication, leadership, and conflict—theory that was relevant for all social workers and particularly for those engaged in group and community work.[16] But at this time social workers were just beginning to enter the academic atmosphere as teachers and their major interdisciplinary contacts were not with social scientists but with other professionals in practice.

It was the work with individuals, rather than community action, that advanced first toward professional formulation, apparently because visible models and useful theory were readily available. Richmond's pioneer formulation of social casework drew from two major professions for its central themes, the concept of social diagnosis from medicine and the concept of social evidence from law. Medicine further provided the clinical model, encompassing study, diagnosis, and treatment.[17] Richmond's formulation is generally regarded as the first authoritative statement in social work, which began to lay the theoretical foundation for the profession.

It is important to understand better how the various forces and influences operated in this formative period. Richmond's analysis directed attention to a clinical model of practice. Soon thereafter, psychoanalytic psychiatry offered a body of theory that social workers found immediately useful. Its focus on individual

---

[16] Georg Simmel, *Sociologie* (Leipzig, Germany: Duncker & Humber, 1908); and Charles H. Cooley, *Social Process* (New York: Charles Scribner's Sons, 1918).

[17] Mary E. Richmond, *Social Diagnosis* (New York: Russell Sage Foundation, 1917).

personality and its therapeutic base were particularly meaningful in relation to casework as a helping process. Emphasis on the emotions directed attention to the psychic aspects of social maladjustment. Since social workers depend mainly upon their direct contact and relationship with others to bring about results, the new theory offered further insight through its concepts of transference and the therapist's role. The fact that social workers were increasingly practicing in association with psychiatrists provided opportunity for constant refreshment of theory and strengthened this trend in social work thinking.

The psychiatric model in turn reinforced the medical model, with its emphasis on treatment. It was a therapeutic approach. The social work goal of helping people thus came to be perceived as a treatment process operating through the client-worker relationship. Since social work did not have disease categories, as did medicine and psychiatry, diagnosis in social casework was directed toward understanding the individual client and his problem. Thus it was expected that every social worker would develop an attitude of acceptance, tolerance, and warmth toward his clients. He would regard the client's feelings, goals, and individual point of view as being of primary importance and make every effort to understand them. He would endeavor to help the client meet his difficulties and solve his problems as far as possible in his own way. He would work with the client as a unique human being.

Therefore, to attain such goals, it became necessary for the social worker to be aware of his own emotional biases and the way in which they block or divert his efforts to help. He needed to be able to develop a professional relationship with the persons being helped, through which they could receive support without being dominated or led into inappropriate dependency, so that they could move toward recognition and use of their own strengths. This approach was then transferred to the educational process. Thus, just as it was necessary for the social worker to individualize the client, it became necessary for the teacher and supervisor to individualize the social work student or young practitioner, so that he could develop the self-discipline required to incorporate these essential attitudes and skills within his professional self. Learning was perceived as taking place primarily through supervised experience. This led to the development of fieldwork and supervision as new professional procedures. Thus the case method and supervision became the major channels of teaching and learning.

As casework evolved, social workers' perceptions became defined in directions that proved important for the whole profession. One was the development of a number of ideas that grew into central concepts in teaching and practice. These were the *self-determination* of the client, the *acceptance* of the client by the worker, the *client-worker relationship,* and the *self-awareness* of the worker. These themes spread beyond casework and, in one form or another, became characteristic of all social work practice. Their importance for the profession is referred to throughout this monograph.

Another direction in which perceptions peculiar to social work thinking were developing was in relation to the concept of method. This seems to have grown primarily out of social workers' perceptions of their ways of helping people, that is, the helping process. In medicine, all physicians used the same diagnostic approach, whatever the disease or health problem. Social workers, however, because they perceived themselves to be working with people who had problems, sought understanding of the client as an individual and the meaning of the problem to him, thus individualizing their approach. The *uniqueness* of the individual was emphasized. The social worker's awareness of his own feelings, his sensitivity to the client's feelings, and his offering of help through the relationship became predominant themes.

A diagnostic approach and treatment technique that involved understanding and working with a unique individual obviously could be relevant only for casework. While personality theory was being taught to all social workers, the particular knowledge required and used in understanding and helping people under stress—regarding their feelings in seeking help, their use of help, and similar aspects—was perceived as a component of casework and incorporated within the method, just as the essential attitudes and skills had been incorporated within the student. Strong emphasis was placed on "feeling and doing," with less recognition for "thinking and knowing."

When group workers and community organization workers began to move toward formulation of their practice principles, they turned to the social sciences for concepts and theory, for by this time other disciplines—particularly sociology, social psychology, and anthropology—had developed theories immediately useful for social work. Group workers and community organization workers selected some of these theories, such as theory related to group process and community forces, and applied them to their own practice. In contrast with caseworkers, who dealt primarily with problems of maladjustment, group workers viewed themselves as entering situations before pathology appeared and were largely concerned with promoting the positive growth of group members (for instance, offering recreational services for adolescents and preparing immigrants for participation in a democratic society). For their part, community organization workers, in their efforts to co-ordinate social services and programs, viewed the community as a whole. These extensions of knowledge, the concern for the positive contribution of social work, and the broadened perception of effort were all relevant and needed in the growing practice of the profession.

Arriving at formulation at a later point than in casework, social workers in group work and community organization had an opportunity to move the profession toward integrative ways of thinking. Perhaps they could have done this through identifying some common aspect of human behavior and social problems with which all social workers are concerned and showing how this could become part of a common body of knowledge for the profession. But instead, they followed the casework model and gave primacy to the way of working with people—the methodological approach. This divided practice into three methods, focused on individuals, groups, and communities. The knowledge for each method was also divided and used separately. Students were taught in separate sequences in schools and in different types of agencies. Thus the social work concept of method developed, which views the method as incorporating its own diagnostic approach, cluster of knowledge, and ways of working with people.[18]

---

[18] See William E. Gordon, "Preliminary Report on Social Work Methods" (New York: NASW Commission on Practice, March 21–23, 1963). (Mimeographed.) Dr. Gordon was then chairman of the Working Definition Subcommittee. The report says: " 'Method of social work' is used by the majority of social workers to include the value, knowledge, and purposes associated with the method." (P. 1.)

Under these circumstances, a basic diagnostic approach for all social workers could not be formulated. Furthermore, no visible body of knowledge was being built up. Much knowledge was being subsumed within the methods, instead of being taught as social work knowledge, general to the profession, applicable as needed, and appropriate in any phase of specific practice. Just as the separate fields of practice had produced fragmentation, so the three separate methods tended to limit and hold social work thinking within the barriers of their respective approaches.

It can now be seen that what had been developing was a model for social work practice based on method and skill.[19] This was not deliberately and consciously developed as a model but had become one, in the sense that it was molding social workers' perceptions of practice through defining a focus and setting limits for their thinking. The primary concern was with the skilled social worker and the methods he used, in other words, a *method-and-skill* model. It was not confined to casework but was followed also in group work and community organization.

We should recognize the strengths of this model. It grew out of a highly responsible effort to meet the needs of people. It produced a sensitive, skillful practitioner and an important group of concepts regarding social work's contribution to clients. We have seen how the qualities and skills to be incorporated in the individual worker—such as respect for people, warmth, acceptance, effort to understand their problems, self-awareness, and a disciplined professional relationship—have become ideal characteristics of the whole profession. The supervisory method was amazingly successful in producing a practitioner who was sensitive to the needs and feelings of those being helped (whether as individuals or groups) and skilled in helping. Social workers rightly prize this aspect of their practice. As the profession broadens and grows, these characteristics should not be lost, for they are at the very core of social work as a helping process.

---

[19] The term *model* is used here according to the following definitions in *Webster's Third New International Dictionary* (Springfield, Mass.: G. & C. Merriam Co., 1961), p. 1451: ". . . 14a: a description, a collection of statistical data, or an analogy used to help visualize often in a simplified way something that cannot be directly observed (as an atom) [and] b: a theoretical projection in detail of a possible system of human relationships (as in economics, politics, or psychology). . . ."

3

barriers to

integrative thinking

The first step in the solution of a problem is to recognize it. Therefore, having discussed social workers' perceptions of their practice, it seems important at this point in the discussion to attempt to identify some of the features of social work thinking that have delayed its growth as a profession and represent hazards for the future. Recognition of these limitations and gaps will provide a clearer focus on the positive aspects of the profession's contribution.

Two characteristics of social workers' thinking about their practice—both outgrowths of the traditional practice—are of particular significance. One is the primary concern with skill and method and the other is the emphasis on "feeling and doing" as against "thinking and knowing." All professions have distinctive methods or ways of delivering their expertise. For helping professions, tying feeling and doing together seems appropriate. It is the way in which these modes of thinking are used, with what emphasis and how related to the essentials of the profession, that becomes crucial.

Anti-intellectual attitudes. There has been considerable comment in recent years on the anti-intellectual attitude that has existed and remains strong in social work. The sources of this attitude are complex and run deep because they seem to be en-

37

meshed with some of the strengths and basic characteristics of the profession. Perhaps the dominant reason has been the focus on the individual—his worth, his dignity, his feelings, and his growth. As indicated earlier, the uniqueness of the individual has been strongly maintained all through social work history. There has been resistance to "breaking him into pieces" through any kind of scientific analysis. "It is the *whole* person to whom the social worker relates" and who must be perceived in his full integrity. Thus one finds in teaching and in the literature a trend that was predominant over a long period, namely, dependence on the single case as a way of understanding and learning.[1] Characteristically, the case was presented first, followed by the theoretical analysis. That generalization cannot follow from a single instance did not seem to affect this pattern of thinking. For the social worker, the reality was the single case that demonstrated the worker's skill in working with a unique individual. What is known and understood from professional experience was felt to emerge best through such fully described examples. As with the concept of relationship, social workers communicated with each other and attained a sense of community through such vivid discussion of their own practice, but development of theory was delayed because generalization was not possible.

Under these circumstances a rigorous intellectual approach associated with scientific thinking is resisted, whether consciously or unconsciously. It is perceived on the one hand as a threat to the uniqueness of the individual. On the other hand, since it seems cold and impersonal, it is perceived as a threat to the skill of the social worker, to the sensitivity and the artistic element that are regarded as so important in social work.

The psychiatric orientation of many social workers, with its emphasis on understanding the irrational aspects of behavior, has probably furthered the anti-intellectual attitude. Thus for some social workers, direct intellectual approaches to understanding and working with people may be dismissed with the derogatory term of "intellectualization."

Resistance to the deductive approach. Barriers to social work

---

[1] Helen Harris Perlman, "The Charge to the Casework Sequence," *Social Work*, Vol. 9, No. 3 (July 1964), pp. 47–55.

thinking also appear in the form of resistance to frames of refer-·
ence and generalizations about social work practice. Such attempts to analyze and describe experience seem to many social
workers as if they are imposed, domineering, and artificial. The
deductive approach is mistrusted. In considering the examination
of practice, social workers frequently assert that they would prefer
to start with some small piece of practice familiar to them and
not become involved in global hypotheses or comprehensive
frames of reference covering the essentials of their practice. A
book review in *Science* quotes Conant on this issue:

> Certainly there are two modes of thought, and perhaps
> more than two, but none of the great scientists and inventors,
> or even philosophers, has ever been exclusively inductive
> or deductive. Both approaches are necessary, but there
> must be some sort of meaningful balance between the two.[2]

Many social workers feel that just by getting close to reality they
can somehow learn and function better. The practice of placing
students in fieldwork as soon as they enter school rests on the
assumption that they will learn through this "real" experience.
It is not recognized that reality itself is a chaos of detail, that
facts and experience alone will never reveal their own meaning,
and that it is only as man brings order into experience through
his own thinking that understanding becomes possible. Conant
explains the relation between facts and concepts in this way:

> The test of a new concept is not only the economy and
> simplicity with which it can accommodate known observa-
> tions, but its fruitfulness. Science has a dynamic quality
> when viewed not as a practical undertaking but as a process
> of developing conceptual schemes. Science advances not
> by the accumulation of new facts (a process which may even
> conceivably retard scientific progress) but by the continuous
> development of new and fruitful concepts. . . . History shows

---

2 Robert B. MacLeod, "Science and Education," review of James Bryant
Conant, *Two Modes of Thought: My Encounters with Science and Educa-
tion* (New York: Trident Press, 1964), in *Science*, Vol. 148, No. 3674
(May 28, 1965), p. 1207.

that only by a continuous development of pure science can the practical arts, including medicine, advance.[3]

Yet in spite of resistance to the deductive approach, social workers have shown overconfidence in limited clusters of theory. Furthermore, even though there is resistance to scientific scrutiny as a threat to individualization, it has been shown that the capacity of practitioners to individualize is often quite limited and stereotypes may be too easily accepted in case diagnosis.[4] An interesting observation, which needs to be better understood, is that social workers have been more ready to accept theory from other disciplines than to submit their own experience to rigorous analysis.

Misuse of the democratic approach. Another factor that has retarded theoretical advance is a misuse of the democratic approach that characterizes—sometimes even burdens—the profession. This attitude emphasizes the freedom of those engaged in thinking about professional matters to proceed in the direction of their own particular interest. Such freedom too often hinders the careful examination of fruitful suggestions and leads to the scattering of ideas. Potentially promising lines of advance are thus sidetracked because professional groups or committees do not recognize their responsibility to develop and continue work in the development of theory and knowledge-building that has gone before. Each group wants to make a fresh start. Unfortunately, this tendency devalues and ignores the need for continuity and consistency of thinking over a long enough period to demonstrate results. Researchers do not seem to test each other's findings as is customary in other professions. The imaginative contribution of the individual is emphasized at the expense of the developing mainstream of the profession.

Current approaches to social action. The increase in social problems is currently producing another kind of emphasis on feel-

---

[3] James Bryant Conant, "The Scientist in Our Unique Society," *The Atlantic*, Vol. 181, No. 3 (March 1948), p. 48.

[4] David Fanshel, "Sources of Strain in Practice-oriented Research," *Social Casework*, Vol. 47, No. 6 (June 1966), pp. 357–362; and Alfred Kadushin, "Diagnosis and Evaluation for (Almost) All Occasions," *Social Work*, Vol. 8, No. 1 (January 1963), pp. 12–19.

ing and doing, which is found in social action and is having a growing influence. The type of social action that is directed primarily toward human rights and immediate action, rather than social planning, is imbued with great emotion. It tends to use methods and measures based on the pressure and power of numbers of people and to devalue—sometimes reject—the knowledge and expertise of the profession. Whereas many of the earlier approaches in social work practice stressed feeling and doing in such a way as to produce a fragmented and restricted kind of thinking, this particular social action approach uses a new combination of feeling and doing that tends toward broadly diffused activity in which some of the essentials of the profession, particularly its knowledge, could be lost.

Partial Approaches and Unintended By-products

Continued concentration on partial phases of a profession's practice without an equally strong effort to develop and sustain bonds with the rest of practice can produce unintended results, which may remain latent over considerable periods before they are recognized.[5] As social workers entered one new agency or setting after another, they were impressed with the need to find an appropriate place within each program. The literature regarding the various fields of practice discusses the specialized nature of the work and the adaptations that social workers must make to the specific practice. The setting, the characteristic social problems, and the specific functions of social workers are usually described, but what is being adapted is not made clear.[6] It is apparently either what social workers learned in schools of social work or some general concept of social work and its practice. Since these assumptions were not made explicit, they failed to provide a firm base for social workers' operation in particular settings. Under these circumstances, social workers employed in complex

---

[5] Elliott Dunlap Smith, "Education and the Task of Making Social Work Professional," *Social Service Review*, Vol. 31, No. 1 (March 1957), pp. 1–10.

[6] *See* the references on fields of practice, footnotes 2–6, Chapter 2, of this book.

42   THE COMMON BASE OF SOCIAL WORK PRACTICE

institutions, such as schools or hospitals, have at times become so involved in simply aiding individuals to deal with the confusing requirements and procedures that they have been diverted from their social work responsibility—that of helping with more significant psychosocial problems.

Others employed in non-social work settings sometimes come to identify with the concepts and goals of other professional groups, such as medicine or psychiatry, more strongly than with those of their own profession. Still other social workers are so placed that they have difficulty keeping in close touch with the people being served. Group workers have a special problem in that they frequently supervise untrained group leaders and thus have relatively little direct contact with group members. Community organizers who work mainly with agency programs may have little opportunity for direct contact with the people who have the problems. In all these circumstances, the complex structure of the situation requires that social workers have a clear concept of their own professional contribution if they are not to be pulled off their own base by the outer pressures and latent forces operating in these environments.

Special hazards for social work have resulted from the emphasis on method and skill described earlier. Technical and skillful operations tend to become more efficient as they move toward better understood—and thus more narrowly defined—problems and situations. Practitioners experience greater satisfaction and security in dealing with a manageable problem; therefore they may unconsciously put the "successful" technique first and seek situations that fit the method.[7] Eventually this can lead (and has led) to a diversion from the primary concern for people in need or from social work values to a pursuit of skill for its own sake. Such a result is particularly likely to occur in a profession like social work, which is at a stage when the perspective is still relatively undefined.

Practitioners educated as caseworkers, group workers, or community organization workers are necessarily in the position of offering their one method as their competence. This leads them to seek people to help who can use their particular kind of service.

---

[7] Alfred J. Kahn, "The Function of Social Work in the Modern World," in Kahn, ed., *Issues in American Social Work* (New York: Columbia University Press, 1959), pp. 6–8.

This in turn produces a situation in which applicants are accepted or rejected by an agency according to whether they fit into the narrowly drawn pattern of those who can be helped by the particular technique or method, or, when accepted, clients may be given only the treatment the agency is prepared to give, whether or not it is most relevant to the clients' problems. Social workers can become frustrated when their skills are not used, as when the "wrong" clients apply to agencies or physicians make "poor" referrals to medical or psychiatric social workers in health agencies. During the period in which intensive counseling through office interviews was emphasized, social caseworkers sought verbal clients who could define their problems and who possessed sufficient ego strengths to make constructive use of the client-worker relationship. Waiting lists, required because of the slowness of the method, became barriers to clients who sought help. The duration and continuity of a case came to be valued for its own sake, while brief contacts were devalued. Under these circumstances, the client had to conform to a narrowly defined agency program, which tended to serve decreasing numbers of individuals in the face of a growing population and mounting socioeconomic needs. It was this practice that led to criticism of social workers and agencies as rigid and alienated from those needing help, particularly the inarticulate poor.[8]

The skills developed through early psychoanalytic theory enabled social workers to follow the client's feelings and deal with transference elements in the professional relationship, thus being helpful to emotionally disturbed clients. Recognition of the unconscious and irrational aspects of human behavior has been an important influence on social work practice, enabling social workers to accept dependent, hostile, and other types of "problem" behavior, to move slowly, to work understandingly with people, and not to expect too much in the way of results. There was satisfaction in observing how the theory really did bring clarification of the behavior of so many of the individuals who came for help with their personal problems to child guidance clinics, family agencies, and other health and welfare agencies.

---

[8] Robert Perlman and David Jones, *Neighborhood Service Centers* (Washington, D.C.: U.S. Department of Health, Education & Welfare, 1967), p. 4.

Such diagnosis involves the assessment of the motivation of another person and identification of the elements in his behavior, such as defenses, of which he is not aware, thus inevitably placing the professional person in a position of superiority. However, unintended results can occur in such a situation. When clients are labeled "regressed" or "infantile," the warmth in the casework relationship can become diluted. When social workers began searching for the "real" problem underlying the simple difficulties so often presented in first interviews, some clients felt this response to be insensitive to their needs and they did not return.

Here was a body of theory with brilliant insights that offered man the first great opportunity in history to break through to an understanding of the hitherto hidden mysteries of his own behavior. It was, however, limited theory, in the sense that it dealt mainly with the psychic aspects of behavior and was of a type not easily subjected to scientific testing. Furthermore, holders of the theory, both psychiatrists and social workers, were likely to describe others who raised questions as "resistant" and thus to use the theory for protection against investigation of its validity. For a while social work practice, dominated by casework, made rapid progress through the use of psychoanalytic theory. In the forties the development of two schools of thought, the "diagnostic" and the "functional," required considerable rethinking, which tended to reinforce the emphasis on skill in the professional relationship and the helping process.[9] By this time the knowledge gap resulting from such heavy dependence on one body of theory had become too great for a growing profession with a scope as wide as social work.

---

[9] The "diagnostic" school, rooted in Freudian psychology, emphasized the social worker's responsibility for understanding the client and his behavior, past and present, and for working with the client to gain a better understanding of his problems, which would lead toward possible ways of dealing with the problems. The "functional" school took the psychology of Rank and his concept of will as its base. It stressed the importance of the client working out his problems in the present situation through the professional relationship with the worker and in relation to agency function. Major disagreement centered around the nature and degree of the worker's responsibility in the problem-solving process. The theoretical conflict led to significant re-examination of casework practice and diminishing difference as time went on.

Other unintended consequences followed from the emphasis on self-awareness and self-discipline in social work practice. The original purpose was to develop a professional worker who would not allow his emotional bias to interfere with his capacity to help his clients, particularly in his management of the client-worker relationship. The development of such awareness through the supervisory process is a complex undertaking. If the teaching emphasized this as a major goal, lacking the balance of a broader social work perspective—as sometimes occurred—such teaching could produce young practitioners who were so concerned with their own professional discipline and "neutrality" that they were unable to respond to the client with the warmth, acceptance, and sensitivity that are essential to social work. The overconcern with one aspect of skill in this way produced the very opposite of what was intended.

Social workers had been taught to listen to the client, to follow his feelings, and to avoid dominating him or taking the problem away from him. Originating in casework, this approach spread throughout the profession and became one of its strengths in working with people. Under some circumstances, however, this approach had unintended results. Social workers extended it to situations other than those relating to clients, that is, to their working relationships with associates, as in planning conferences in agencies or the community. They tended to work indirectly toward facilitating the contribution of others but avoided their own direct contribution. In multidisciplinary conferences in the health setting, social workers too often sat passively, waiting for others to speak. Since physicians expect professional personnel to make contributions to the team discussion, they were puzzled by this passive behavior and commented on it. Obviously, in a world full of social innovation and change, social workers could have little impact on situations through such an approach. They require greater confidence in their own contribution and greater initiative in presenting it.

These manifestations, described here as unintended results, illustrate what Schorr calls "the retreat to the technician," a situation in which a narrow focus on technique and skill actually obscures the essential and primary concern for the people who need help and for the broad objectives of the profession.[10] It is a phenomenon of professionalism, of professional development gone awry. It can occur in mature professions but is less likely to occur in those having a strong, well-recognized base.

Lack of Social Work Concepts

The effective operation of a profession rests on a body of common symbols, ideas, and concepts through which the practice can be described and the practitioners can communicate with each other. One of the problems in social work has been the lack of adequate words, terms, and concepts to represent the important facets and components of the profession's practice as a whole.

One significant gap was the lack of a single term to encompass all the measures used by the profession for dealing with psychosocial problems. This resulted in the attempt to extend casework concepts to other areas of practice. Frequently found in the literature are such phrases as "treatment of the community as client." But both "client" and "treatment" are misleading when used in such a broad context. Client inevitably conveys the idea of working through direct contact or a relationship. Treatment carries with it all the shades of meaning from general medicine and psychiatry, which imply the activity of a professional who will diagnose the pathology of the individual and direct action toward alleviation or cure. Casework, in spite of movement toward emphasizing ego strengths, has continued to emphasize the offering of treatment to disturbed, regressed, and "sick" individuals and to place the problem predominantly within the personality. A term is required that will not have therapeutic implications and not be tied to the three methods.

Broader and more positive terms are needed to describe social work practice. The initiative, potential, and independence of the persons to be served require greater recognition. Finding "client" unsatisfactory, this monograph uses the phrase "people involved in the situation or problem." This is an awkward phrase to manage

---

[10] Alvin L. Schorr, "The Retreat to the Technician," *Social Work*, Vol. 4, No. 1 (January 1959), pp. 29–33.

but avoids the undesirable connotations. In the same way, the term "situation" is used instead of "case," since the latter carries the implication of work with individuals.

Another trend in thinking is to be noted. In the last decade or two, writers about the social work profession and its practice and committees working on professional problems have tended to seek to identify the issues as the best means for understanding a situation. One wonders if this trend is influenced by the growing concern about social problems and social policy, since in the political area difference of opinion is a major characteristic. In a profession or scientific discipline, however, the best avenue toward understanding is usually considered to be the identification of phenomena, conditions, or situations and the relationship between them. This is an orderly approach in which understanding comes before action. The concept of issues, on the other hand, has built into it the idea of controversy and debate. Both types of concepts are needed in a profession like social work, to be used in their proper contexts.

In the face of a complex reality, social workers perceive more clearly and communicate with each other best regarding those entities that have been clearly conceptualized. Those parts of reality that are not conceptualized, even though they may be important for well-rounded thinking, remain as gaps in the general structure of thought. Thus social work's progress has been delayed and blocked by the fact that for so long there were no adequate comprehensive concepts, and thus no consistent words or terms, to describe the profession's central focus, the people whom it serves, and its ways of helping. In the long run, it is more important to build a viable theoretical structure for the profession as a whole than to be swayed by political currents and academic fashions of the moment.

part two
professional model
for social work
practice

4

a professional model
for social work practice

An impression gained from a general view of social work growing through its parts, as described earlier, is that there was much in this practice in fields and agencies and in this use of methods and skill that could and would contribute to a common professional base. But, until such a base was established, fragmentation of practice would continue.

In its early period the *method-and-skill* model led to creative thinking. Skill, self-awareness, and defined method are essential for a profession. But they are not adequate in themselves to provide a complete professional base. Practitioners in various areas of practice had been provided with a set of ideas that were limited but just workable enough to get along with. Because of their partial and separate frames of reference, however, different groups of practitioners emphasized different approaches. The original conceptualization of practice identified the three methods as separate entities—casework, group work, and community organization. Practitioners were expected to be competent in and use one or the other. In the schools, the curriculum offered (and required) concentration in one method; thus students followed different tracks. Because the emphasis on skill in fieldwork predominated over the emphasis on basic knowledge and theory in the classroom, graduates emerged who regarded themselves primarily as "casework-

51

ers," "group workers," or "community organization workers." The idea that they were all social workers received less recognition. In a profession that still lacked unity, it was more comfortable to practice in a defined area. Some of the best thinking was done in the separate practice areas or in an educational framework related to them. However, method—unless disturbed by some radical force—tends toward ever greater technical precision and increasing narrowness of focus. Thus social workers worked at refining their own areas but were prevented by the barriers between the methods from communicating easily with each other regarding the area of common concern—social work practice as a comprehensive concept. They tended to criticize each other for being too one-sided in one direction or another without perceiving how they could all move together toward a unified perspective.

From time to time, efforts to counteract the divisive trends in practice were made. As early as 1929, the Milford Conference (a voluntary committee of social workers concerned with the analysis and clarification of social casework) developed the "generic-specific" concept, which advanced the idea of a generic base underlying the practice of casework in the specific fields. The generic part of the concept encouraged the unification of casework and the growth of the generic curriculum in schools, but the whole concept proved too complex for effective application throughout practice at that early stage in the profession's development.[1] In the mid-fifties, following a decision to discontinue the teaching of specialization by fields in the schools, the Council on Social Work Education requested representatives of the fields of practice to examine their practice and report what content in terms of particular knowledge, skills, and attitudes they considered basic for all social workers and what, in addition, was essential to competence for workers practicing in their specific fields.[2] Another effort was made shortly thereafter by the National Association of

---

[1] *Social Case Work, Generic and Specific* (New York: American Association of Social Workers, 1929); and Harriett M. Bartlett, "The Generic-Specific Concept in Social Work Education and Practice," in Alfred J. Kahn, ed., *Issues in American Social Work* (New York: Columbia University Press, 1959), pp. 159–190.

[2] "Description of Practice Statements: Fields of Social Work Practice" (New York: Council on Social Work Education, 1959). (Mimeographed.)

Social Workers, which submitted to the various fields a set of questions suggesting criteria for identifying characteristics common to all the fields of practice.[3] Although these projects stimulated integrative thinking about social work practice, they did not succeed in attaining the kind of agreement about common elements that was needed and sought.

Need for a Professional Model

Eventually, by the fifties, the liabilities of a fragmented approach to practice rose to the surface. The skilled professional worker could perform helpfully in serving clients. Teachers and practitioners of high caliber were writing with great self-awareness about their practice and teaching in social work journals. But because of the emphasis on "the uniqueness of the individual," "the case," and "the specific situation," generalizations were not emerging from practice experience in any significant number. Some important aspects of practice, such as the professional relationship with clients, had been thoroughly examined but others—such as the nature of social work knowledge—had received relatively little attention. Growth of theory was held back and the professional literature was not developing in cumulative fashion.[4] In 1959, Hearn commented that a point of diminishing return in the building of social work practice theory seemed to have been reached.[5] Other observers noted that practicing workers lacked awareness of the knowledge on which their practice rested.[6] Since the professional attributes of social workers were thus obscured, they were not well understood by other collaborating professions or society in general. The profession was at the point at which it had to certify the competence of its members in society but, because

---

[3] NASW Commission on Social Work Practice, Subcommittee on Fields of Practice, "Identifying Fields of Practice in Social Work," *Social Work,* Vol. 7, No. 2 (April 1962), pp. 7–14.

[4] Roger W. Little, "The Literature of Social Casework," *Social Casework,* Vol. 33, No. 7 (July 1952), pp. 287–291.

[5] Gordon Hearn, *Theory Building in Social Work* (Toronto, Canada: University of Toronto Press, 1958), p. 23.

[6] William E. Gordon, "Toward a Social Work Frame of Reference," *Journal of Education for Social Work,* Vol. 1, No. 2 (Fall 1965), p. 23.

of the manner in which skill had been conceptualized, an authoritative formulation and consensus regarding the essentials of this competence were not available. Commenting on restrictive legal regulation in 1962, the National Association of Social Workers said in an official statement that it did not favor such action at that time, "since the social work profession is not ready to define the activities that comprise social work practice in a way that sets forth the common elements in all practice, the boundaries of practice, and the distinguishing elements." [7] Recognition was growing that the old view of practice was outworn; a real breakthrough in thinking was needed.

Important changes in social work as a whole were stimulating new ways of looking at practice. In the late forties, convinced that in order to develop a profession they must form a united professional organization, social workers embarked on six years of exploration and planning. In 1955, the separate practice organizations came together and the National Association of Social Workers, a new membership organization, was established. This step—the formation of a comprehensive, united professional organization—made it possible to deal with social work practice as a whole, with a clarity not previously possible in social work history. From this broadened perception emerged a new, comprehensive model for practice, based on the general model of a profession. This model assumes that a profession possesses a body of theoretical, ethical, and technical principles that is conveyed to its students and practitioners through educational channels in the form of generalizations and principles. The practitioner's actions are guided by these generalizations and principles, which he applies to individual situations in his practice. [8]

On first acquaintance, the *method-and-skill* model and the *professional* model appear similar. Both revolve around a "social worker in action," but the difference is that in the latter model the worker's action is placed within a general social work frame of reference and perspective and is consciously guided by the broadly

---

[7] "Legal Regulation of Social Work Practice," *NASW News,* Vol. 7, No. 2 (February 1962), p. 9.

[8] *See* the discussion of the concept of a profession, pp. 18–20 of this book.

defined values, knowledge, and techniques of the whole profession.[9] The implications of this distinction are far reaching. A profession is customarily described as a combination of art and science. The art is demonstrated in the performance of the individual practitioner; the science is found in the profession's body of knowledge and ways of thinking. A profession is recognized as growing stronger as the scientific component in its knowledge and thinking is increased. Every profession must find the balance between its science and its art that will enable it to grow and improve the effectiveness of its service in society.[10]

It is the art rather than the science of the profession that has been developed primarily by the method-and-skill model in social work. The central concept is one of a helping service. The focus is therapeutic, on treatment goals and professional skill in treatment processes. The worker is expected to incorporate the essential attitudes and skills. Feeling and doing, rather than knowing and thinking, are emphasized, and theory is taught in such a way as to be integrated directly with feeling and doing. In this model, thinking is usually not emphasized or taught in practice as a distinct process that is of value in bringing understanding and order into complex situations.[11] This approach leads to the social work concept of method, which ties knowledge and value

---

[9] The reader will find that sometimes value is used in the singular and sometimes in the plural. No special intent is implied by either usage, but in general when the subject is discussed in the abstract, along with knowledge, purpose, and other basic components of a profession, we use *value* (the singular). When we are discussing the subject in more specific terms, such as the use of values in practice, we use *values* (the plural). Examination of the literature shows that past usage has been inconsistent and that the connotations attached to the singular and plural still have to be worked out in terms of their philosophical implications.

[10] Joseph W. Eaton, "Science, 'Art,' and Uncertainty in Social Work," *Social Work*, Vol. 3, No. 3 (July 1958), pp. 3–10.

[11] It is now recognized that this concentration on the individual student or practitioner and his learning through direct experience unduly prolonged the apprenticeship method of teaching in social work. *See* Walter L. Kindelsperger, "Observations from a Social Work Educator," *Potentials and Problems in the Changing School-Agency Relationships in Social Work Education* (New York: Council on Social Work Education, 1967), pp. 6–14.

to skill and technique. Thus the essential professional elements do not stand out clearly in social work practice and the outline of the professional practice itself is blurred.

The two practice models result from viewing practice from different approaches—that of the individual worker and that of the profession. In one sense, these can be regarded as different levels of definition and description. Actually, both approaches are needed and should not be separated. In fact, many social workers have been pointing out that the practice of the skilled worker would be stronger and more effective if based on a systematic body of knowledge and value.

The reasons why social work moved so far without giving more attention to its body of knowledge and values need to be understood. Probably this was due to the very success of the method-and-skill model over a long period. Sensitive teachers and supervisors seem to have been able to transmit to students and young workers, and to develop in them through direct personal communication and example, a high proportion of the capacities and attitudes desired in the professional practitioner. It is remarkable that this should have been carried so far while central concepts, such as self-determination and acceptance or relationship and support, still lacked definitive formulation.

As time went on, many questions were being raised by social workers themselves. Why have we developed this narrow focus in a period of broad social change? Where is the profession's body of knowledge? What is the central contribution of social work to society? From what perspective is this developed?

What is now needed for the profession's forward movement is not to discard the method-and-skill model as a whole, but to carry over from it those aspects that are contributing to the strengths of social work and to include them in the new professional model. In this way, the concept of the skilled worker can take its proper place within a comprehensive concept of social work and its practice. The method-and-skill model needs greater breadth, while the overall professional model needs substance. The problem is to find how these limitations can be overcome and how an effective integration can be achieved that combines the strengths of both.

A Professional Model ("The Working Definition")

In earlier years, writers like Pray began to develop integrative ideas about social work; but when the National Association of Social Workers was formed in 1955, no general frame of reference for viewing practice was available.[12]   A newly organized Commission on Socal Work Practice, needing such a formulation as a base for its program, set forth what it called a "Working Definition of Social Work Practice."   Single brief definitions of social work had, of course, been attempted in the past by individuals and groups.   The Working Definition differed from these in that it was conceived as an ongoing undertaking, to which many people would contribute and that would keep evolving as the profession itself grew and matured.   An initial formulation was completed by a special subcommittee in 1958.[13]

At the same time, another helpful formulation appeared in the literature in the form of a general statement regarding the nature of social work prepared by Boehm as part of a comprehensive study of social work education.[14]   This statement gave encouragement because of its agreement with the practice commission formulation, particularly in relation to values and goals.   Because of its educational orientation, the Boehm statement placed less emphasis on defining practice.

The Working Definition is a promising beginning toward a comprehensive professional model for social work practice and is important because it attempts to view all social work practice and to do this from the viewpoint of the profession.   Our analysis of previous thinking shows why this is a much-needed advance for social work and a significant step in its growth.

Since the Working Definition was the beginning of an ongoing stream of thinking about social work practice, it is worthwhile for

---

12 Kenneth L. M. Pray, *Social Work in a Revolutionary Age* (Philadelphia: University of Pennsylvania Press, 1949).

13 "Working Definition of Social Work Practice," *Social Work,* Vol. 3, No. 2 (April 1958), pp. 5–8. *See* full copy of the Working Definition in the Appendix, pp. 221–224 of this book.

14 Werner W. Boehm, "The Nature of Social Work," *Social Work,* Vol. 3, No. 2 (April 1958), pp. 10–18.

our purposes to review the history of the statement and also to consider the further development of the ideas it contains. According to the original plan, the formulation would be revised from time to time, but at this time of writing, no actual revision has been completed. However, a number of articles on the subject, based on the work of a second subcommittee under the chairmanship of William E. Gordon and by others who participated in the original effort, have been published. Readers should keep in mind that it is necessary to be familiar with the continuing discussion on the Working Definition in the social work literature in order to understand the developing concepts and their full implications.[15]

The first question before the Subcommittee on the Working Definition of Social Work Practice was: What are we defining? Confusion had arisen in the past because the concept of social work was used in relation to such a wide array of activities within the broad field of social welfare, including activities of personnel other than social workers as well as the programs and services of social agencies. It was agreed that this definition was concerned with the profession of social work and was to focus on practice. This distinction offered an entity to be studied that was broad enough to cover the basic components in practice and yet could be viewed objectively.

The next question had to do with the building of a frame of reference. What should be its components? In a helping profession these are usually identified as value, purpose, knowledge, and method or technique. As used in the original Working Definition, this framework has proved stimulating and useful for further thinking.

A central concept, developed early, was that the elements that

---

[15] Harriett M. Bartlett, "Toward Clarification and Improvement of Social Work Practice," *Social Work,* Vol. 3, No. 2 (April 1958), pp. 3–9; Bartlett, *Analyzing Social Work Practice by Fields* (New York: National Association of Social Workers, 1961); William E. Gordon, "A Critique of the Working Definition," *Social Work,* Vol. 7, No. 4 (October 1962), pp. 3–13; Gordon, "Knowledge and Value: Their Distinction and Relationship in Clarifying Social Work Practice," *Social Work,* Vol. 10, No. 3 (July 1965), pp. 32–39; and Gordon, "Toward a Social Work Frame of Reference," pp. 19–26.

guide the social worker's action form a constellation. "Some social work practice," said the definition, "will show a more extensive use of one or the other of the components but it is social work practice only when they are all present to some degree."[16] Thus there is appropriate variation in the use of the elements but they are consistently present as the essential elements that identify the practice as that of social work. Combining the ideas about the profession and about practice, the core idea became the action of the practitioner directed to a purpose and guided by values, knowledge, and techniques, all of which would have to be described in social work terms.[17]

A profession's purposes are in general directed toward fulfilling the outcomes implied in its values. Therefore, in social work the overall purpose would be to further the maximum realization of each individual's potential and other purposes would be related to this in some consistent manner. Knowledge is also related to purpose, since at any particular time the available knowledge makes certain goals more practical and attainable than others. Thus value and knowledge interact in determining the professional goals that will be dominant and operative in practice from one period to another. Because of this close relation of purpose to value and knowledge and in order to concentrate on a few major elements, purpose will not be emphasized as a separate element of practice in this discussion.

The concept of *sanction* was included in the original definition to cover the auspices under which practice is carried on. Sanction refers to the authorization that is accorded to social work practice by society, the law, the agency or program, and the professional association itself. Later consideration by the NASW subcommittee, however, suggested that sanction is not a basic definer of social work practice in the same sense as the other essential elements and operates differently from them.[18] It is, therefore, omitted from the frame of reference used in this monograph. Some of its aspects that have to do with the manner in

---

[16] *See* the Working Definition in the Appendix, p. 221.
[17] Gordon, "A Critique of the Working Definition," p. 5.
[18] *Ibid.*, p. 12.

which the program influences the nature of social work practice will be considered in later chapters.

Through the formulation developed in the Working Definition, knowledge and value are made clearly visible, separated from method, and placed in their proper position as basic in a profession. Significant progress is made in offsetting the disproportionate emphasis on method and skill that characterized social work practice in earlier years. Method, which follows value and knowledge in the definition, is already moving away from the particular connotation given to it in the three-methods concept. It is presented as a basic concept in social work practice and is not tied to or divided among the separate methods. While the concept itself is vague, it at least permits freedom for a new approach.

A number of ideas that are only briefly mentioned in the Working Definition assume significance because they indicate a trend and are a starting point for further thinking. The original statement does not discuss where the central concern of social work is to be found nor does it indicate the need for recognizing such a focus; but it does state that the practitioner is concerned with the "interaction between the individual and his social environment with a continuing awareness of the reciprocal effects of one upon the other." Other sections of the formulation indicate that the idea is to be extended to groups. While skill is emphasized, the responsibility of the practitioner for "systematic observation and assessment of the individual or group in a situation" and for "professional judgment" is clearly stated.[19]

As a beginning formulation, the original Working Definition took a major step toward the clarification of social work practice. It identified the essential elements of a profession—value, knowledge, and techniques—and showed how they guide the social worker in his practice. These *essential* elements can be regarded as *basic* social work elements in the sense that (1) they must be present in any "piece" of social work practice and (2) they are *common,* that is, shared by all practitioners. Because, in the writer's opinion, the need for integrative thinking is to be regarded as an overriding concern of social work at this time, the

---

[19] *See* the Working Definition in the Appendix.

second aspect—that the basic elements are common and shared—is being emphasized here. We start from the idea expressed by the second subcommittee on the Working Definition, that "the essence of the professional in his practice must derive from the *shared* values, knowledge, and methods of the profession" and will consider further in this monograph how the thinking about the common elements can be developed and used to strengthen social work and its practice.[20]

At present, many practitioners have not been prepared to think in this way, not having been taught in the past to think in terms of an overall perspective for their practice, not hearing it discussed in meetings, and not encountering it in the literature. Subjects discussed in books and papers have customarily been particular aspects of practice, such as the client-worker relationship, group leadership, and agency co-ordination, or social welfare problems like the means test. Only recently has material begun to appear in the literature and in teaching in which social workers discuss the common elements in practice in the sense intended here. In 1962 the writer made an exploratory effort to describe the characteristics of social work as far as they could be perceived.[21] The formulation presented in this monograph regarding the common elements attempts a more comprehensive analysis than has been tried before.

---

[20] Gordon, "A Critique of the Working Definition," p. 8.

[21] Harriett M. Bartlett, "Characteristics of Social Work," *Building Social Work Knowledge: Report of a Conference* (New York: National Association of Social Workers, 1964), pp. 1–15.

essential elements
in social work practice

The Working Definition had no sooner been formulated than it gave rise to searching questions. It forced social workers to look directly at questions regarding the basic characteristics and components of social work practice that had not been faced previously because of the preoccupation with partial aspects of practice. In fact, contrary to expectation, the significance of the definition proved to be less in the formulation itself than in the vigorous process of thinking about professional practice that it stimulated. As chairman of the NASW Commission on Social Work Practice, the writer still recalls vividly the sense of excitement and discovery that prevailed among the participants during those early days of exploration.

Values and Knowledge

The original definition included a listing of values, knowledge areas, and techniques. In subsequent discussions, a second sub-committee on the Working Definition recognized the inadequacy of such lists of components and the need for a more searching examination of the nature of each element as well as their relationship to each other. The committee recognized that mature professions rest on strong bodies of knowledge and values from which scientific and ethical principles that guide the operation of the practitioner are derived. In this sense, knowledge and value take priority over method and are the major definers of method and technique.[1]

In studying the Working Definition, the committee found that social workers have confused knowledge and values. Thus the relationship, and particularly the *distinction,* between knowledge and values required further interpretation in clarifying social work practice. Values, the committee said, refer to what is regarded as good and desirable. These are qualitative judgments; they are not empirically demonstrable. They are invested with emotion and represent a purpose or goal toward which the social worker's action will be directed. Knowledge propositions, on the other hand, refer to verifiable experience and appear in the form of rigorous statements that are made as objective as possible. Value statements refer to what is preferred; knowledge statements to what is confirmed or confirmable. In the original Working Definition, for example, a statement that "there is interdependence between individuals in this society" was included under values. It is obvious, however, that this is a demonstrable fact, which should not be classified as a value.[2]

At any stage in the development of scientific knowledge there are some propositions that do not appear confirmable and thus must be regarded as value assumptions. In some instances, however, statements that are identical in form can be taken as either part of knowledge or as values. The idea that home is the best place for a child is an example; it can be taken as preferred or as a hypothesis for investigation. Here it is the *intention* regarding the proposition, rather than its actual substance, that makes the difference. There is also a long-range shift that will take place between a profession's body of knowledge and values. As

---

[1] William E. Gordon, "A Critique of the Working Definition," *Social Work,* Vol. 7, No. 4 (October 1962), p. 12.

[2] William E. Gordon, "Knowledge and Value: Their Distinction and Relationship in Clarifying Social Work Practice," *Social Work,* Vol. 10, No. 3 (July 1965), pp. 32–35.

scientific knowledge increases, some propositions that were at first preferred assumptions will become established as confirmed knowledge. Social conditions that were visualized as desirable may become established in society through social change.[3]

At any one time in a profession's development, teachers, practitioners, and researchers should be clear as to the difference between value and knowledge, and the status of any particular proposition. Knowledge and value play distinctly different roles, both of which are needed. For instance, a social worker may become so committed to the value of self-determination that he concentrates his efforts on what he considers to be the freedom to grow for the children in the families he is serving and thus fails to seek out and use knowledge about the important role of parental discipline in personality development. Here a value is being used as a guide when knowledge also is needed. Conversely, in a controversial situation regarding the direction an agency program should take, an administrator bases his decision on criteria for efficient operation; whereas events later prove that social work values regarding the needs of disadvantaged groups in the community would have been a better guide in this specific situation. Thus it is important to recognize the distinction between knowledge and value and the appropriate use of each in practice.

Proper use of knowledge and value rests not only on distinguishing those propositions that belong in different categories but also in recognizing that the user's intent—whether as a preferred or a confirmable statement—also makes a difference as to how they should be classified.[4] According to this approach, propositions regarded as verifiable by science and research—and that are intended to be verified—are considered to be knowledge. Some people object to including within the profession's knowledge propositions that have not been validated. However, such propositions should certainly not be regarded as values. It seems better to include in a profession's knowledge those propositions that are being used by practitioners but have as yet only the rough testing of practice, along with the propositions validated through rigorous testing. Eventually, those that cannot be verified may

3 *Ibid.*, pp. 35–36.
4 *Ibid.*, pp. 36–37.

have to be discarded. Teachers and practitioners should, of course, be aware when they are dealing with "soft" or "hard" knowledge.

The Value Element

Social work thinking about values is so frequently interwoven with discussion of other elements in practice that a comprehensive and authoritative formulation is not available. Probably the oldest and most widely held value in social work asserts the worth and dignity of every human being. Of increasing importance in social work thinking is another value that has been expressed variously as "self-determination," "self-fulfillment," or "self-realization." The subcommittee on the Working Definition expressed it as "*maximum realization of each individual's potential for development throughout his lifetime.*" [5] In simple terms, it is good for every individual to realize his potential for growth as fully as possible.

Since all individuals are concerned, their needs must be balanced against each other. Therefore, in fulfilling his own potential, each person has the responsibility to help others realize themselves in the same way. Another value, which follows from the rest, asserts the right of individuals to be different from each other. This is of particular importance in today's society, with its pressures toward conformity.

The concept of *potential* is receiving more and more attention and is moving toward the forefront in social work discussion about values. For a long period self-determination was the preferred term and is still in active use, but increased understanding of the manner in which human growth takes place through social interaction indicates its limitations. Self-determination appropriately emphasizes the individual but separates him too much from others. [6] The concept of potential places man within the overall process of evolution on this planet. Because of the nature of cultural evolution, man has both increasing control over his

---

[5] *Ibid.*, p. 38.

[6] Saul Bernstein, "Self-Determination: King or Citizen in the Realm of Values?" *Social Work*, Vol. 5, No. 1 (January 1960), pp. 3–8.

66 THE COMMON BASE OF SOCIAL WORK PRACTICE

growth and a corresponding responsibility for the direction of the process.

As Dubos points out, man is the creature who can choose, eliminate, assemble, decide, and thereby create.[7] Some social workers may prefer to define the directions in which the potential should be realized. Others may prefer not to attempt a definition of specific normative values and goals. "The faith that man when freed can be trusted to grow and develop in desirable directions is probably the highest expression of a belief in human dignity. . . ." [8] Thus, taken as a value proposition, attainment of human potential becomes a good in itself.

A second major theme that emerges from the values preferred by social workers is *growth*. Only through continuous growth can the individual attain his full potential. He gains strength by being given freedom and support to solve his own problems. Respect for his striving is essential. One of the core themes throughout social work history has been that the individual should be given the opportunity to grow in his own way. While other professions emphasize human potential and growth, social work's emphasis on the individual's right to be himself and solve his problems in his own way, with such help and opportunity as are needed, is giving these values a meaning that is characteristic of the social work profession.[9]

As we review these interrelated values, the central position of the individual in the social work value system becomes clear. This is sometimes misunderstood to mean an emphasis on casework, but they are not the same thing. Self-fulfillment and realization of potential for individuals can be furthered by working

---

[7] René Dubos, "Humanistic Biology," *The American Scholar,* Vol. 34, No. 2 (Spring 1965), p. 196.

[8] Gordon, "Knowledge and Value: Their Distinction and Relationship in Clarifying Social Work Practice," p. 38.

[9] *See* Bertha C. Reynolds, "Social Case Work: What Is It? What Is Its Place in the World Today?" pp. 136–137, Charlotte Towle, "Factors in Treatment," pp. 321 and 326, and Gordon Hamilton, "Basic Concepts in Social Case Work," p. 158, in Fern Lowry, ed., *Readings in Social Case Work: 1920–1938* (New York—Columbia University Press, 1939); Gordon Hamilton, "Helping People—The Growth of a Profession," *Social Casework,* Vol. 29, No. 8 (October 1948), pp. 294–295; and Gordon Hearn, *Theory Building in Social Work* (Toronto, Canada: University of Toronto Press, 1958), p. 36.

with groups, communities, and national programs. In contrast with a totalitarian philosophy, which gives priority to the state, the democratic ideal demands a commitment to the welfare of every citizen. It is in this sense that social work places the individual in the center of its concern.

There has been much confusion in the profession on this point. Social workers are often involved in situations in which the good of the individual conflicts with the good of others. How can the issues be resolved when the need of the community for finer buildings and roads runs counter to the need of elderly persons to continue living in a neighborhood in which they feel secure? Or when the need of citizens for protection from crime seems opposed to the need of the individual delinquent for greater understanding and opportunity? Pumphrey suggests that social work's commitment to both the individual and general good calls for a capacity to find a balance between them.[10] Thus the manner in which values relating to the individual and society intermesh in social work's value system needs particular clarification.

Another important characteristic of the social work value orientation is that growth and potential, as expressed in the value of self-fulfillment, are future directed. Out of this fact emerge implications that are only beginning to be recognized. Social workers have always been concerned with the individual's life goals, but psychoanalytic theory turned attention to the causes of his behavior, that is, to the past. Elaborate clinical studies were made as a means of understanding motivation and planning treatment. Now, however, in examining the efforts of individuals and those around them to solve the problems that impede their functioning, more attention is being given to the consequences of these efforts for the individual's growth. The devastating effect of social conditions and social change in blocking the life goals of so many persons in this society directs attention to the need for creating social conditions within which people's efforts and their potential can have greater opportunity for fulfillment. Actually, social workers have always been characteristically concerned with the consequences of people's efforts to deal with their

---

[10] Muriel W. Pumphrey, *The Teaching of Values and Ethics in Social Work Education* (New York: Council on Social Work Education, 1959), p. 43.

difficulties and with the impact of the social environment upon their functioning. Social work's emphasis on growth as a value reinforces this concern for consequences and future outcomes.

It should be clear that when we refer to professional values in this discussion we mean the ethical concepts and principles identified by the profession itself.[11] These are to be distinguished from the cultural value system, which includes the mores and expectations regarding individual and social behavior in society.

It should be further clear that the values are the principles themselves. Some social workers classify as values all aspects of their profession that they regard as particularly important because they "value" them. Under these circumstances items of knowledge or technique, such as "the family as a unit in society" or "the client-worker relationship" may be listed as values. This is probably one reason for the confusion between knowledge and value discussed previously.[12]

Values are frequently divided into ultimate values, which are abstract concepts of what should be, and ideas concerning means to achieve these values, often referred to as instrumental values.[13] As professions develop their values, one or more may emerge as ultimate values. For example, in medicine the attainment of health in the fullest measure for all individuals and the obligation to expend every effort to save life would be examples of such ultimate values and obligations. It may be that social work will move toward attainment of human potential as its ultimate value. Other values are then derived from and related to the overall value or values. The responsibility for each other's growth leads to the recognition that society has the responsibility to remove obstacles and to provide opportunity for individual growth. Such responsibility particularly inheres in a democratic society. Because of the dependence of individual growth upon social relationships and social organization, social workers are committed to democratic principles and the right of groups to function in such a society. Both the responsibility of groups to contribute

---

[11] *See* the Code of Ethics of the National Association of Social Workers.
[12] Gordon, "Knowledge and Value: Their Distinction and Relationship in Clarifying Social Work Practice."
[13] Pumphrey, *op. cit.,* pp. 40–41.

to social welfare and their opportunity to do so are stressed. Other derivative values are developed in the same manner.

Pumphrey points out the need to understand better what values actually operate in guiding practice and at what levels of abstraction. In her examination of the teaching of values, she observed that middle-range or instrumental values were most frequently used in the discussion of practice.[14] Confidentiality, for instance, is a value of this type frequently used by social workers. At present many values that are related to intermediate social goals, like better community participation or strengthened family life, are only loosely related to each other and to the ultimate values of social work. As steps are taken to define the manner in which ultimate and instrumental values are related to each other in a logical system appropriate to social work's way of thinking, movement toward an integrated value system will occur. The Working Definition and concurrent influences in social work education and practice are stimulating interest in such clarification. Thus the profession is taking steps to build its visible body of values.

The Knowledge Element

Ordinarily, a profession's strongest foundation is its body of knowledge. As social work progressively defines its central focus and purposes, its knowledge will be built around them. In the past knowledge has appeared mainly in the form of separate clusters of concepts and theory tied to various areas of practice. There has been mounting concern, evident in many articles in the professional literature, over the slow pace in developing a systematic body of knowledge and the hazard to the profession resulting from this lag has been repeatedly stressed.[15] As with values, the Working Definition has stimulated ongoing efforts to explore ways in which social workers can contribute more directly

---

[14] *Ibid.*, pp. 46–47.

[15] Alfred J. Kahn, "The Nature of Social Work Knowledge," in Cora Kasius, ed., *New Directions in Social Work* (New York: Harper & Bros., 1954), pp. 194–214; and Alfred Kadushin, "The Knowledge Base of Social Work," in Alfred J. Kahn, ed., *Issues in American Social Work* (New York: Columbia University Press, 1959), pp. 39–79.

to knowledge-building, and similar steps are being taken in the schools of social work.[16]

For a long while, what social workers knew was so intermingled with their values and skills that the idea of a separate body of social work knowledge seemed neither useful nor important. With increasing recognition that the maturing profession must have such knowledge, the question of how a profession like social work goes about building its body of knowledge had to be faced. Rich sources of knowledge are available from many directions. The problem is one of identifying, formulating, systematizing, and testing the concepts and generalizations appropriate and meaningful for the profession. Social work shares with many other professions and disciplines the difficulties inherent in the complex, diffuse nature of its subject matter—human behavior. These intricate human events will not fall into order by themselves. Each profession and discipline must find its own way of organizing its knowledge, a way that is most useful for its purposes.[17]

Knowledge from Other Fields

How, then, is social work moving toward this process of knowledge-building? In consciously seeking theory to guide their practice, social workers first turn to outside sources. The largest and most visible portion of knowledge comes from other professions, like medicine, and from academic disciplines, most particularly the behavioral and biological sciences. Concepts and theory are selected from these sources for their relevance to social work, tested in practice, and perhaps extended or reformulated in social work terms. It is customary for professions to borrow in this way from other sources whose knowledge is relevant for their practice, often adding to and enriching the knowledge through such application.

---

16 *Building Social Work Knowledge: Report of a Conference* (New York: National Association of Social Workers, 1964); and Merlin Taber and Iris Shapiro, "Social Work and Its Knowledge Base: A Content Analysis of the Periodical Literature," *Social Work,* Vol. 10, No. 4 (October 1965), pp. 100–106.

17 *Building Social Work Knowledge: Report of a Conference.*

Coyle points out two problems inherent in interprofessional borrowing. The first lies in the acceptance of the theories on the basis of the other profession's authority, particularly if it has high prestige. Under these circumstances there is the possibility that the theory may be accepted as dogma. The second danger lies in the confusion of identification and function that so often seems to result from interprofessional borrowing.[18]

When a whole body of scientific knowledge is relevant to the practice of a profession, the educational system is sometimes developed in the form of a two-layer structure consisting of basic sciences and professional courses, as in the example of medicine.[19] Having available as yet no fully developed social science that can be used in this way, social workers have borrowed either single concepts or small clusters of knowledge and theory from other fields. Finding security in one cluster of theory (as in the instance of psychoanalytic theory), they concentrated excessively on such a single body of knowledge until its limitations were recognized. Then came a swing toward social science in an effort to restore balance. As a result of such unco-ordinated movement, the various concepts and clusters of theory have remained separate, predominantly used by different groups of social workers, such as those trained in casework or community organization. Concepts that would bring together the various facets of behavior with which social work is concerned have not been readily found.

It is the thesis of this discussion that such fragmentation of knowledge will continue to occur until recognition of the essential elements in social work is strong enough to hold the profession more strongly together. Ego psychology, role theory, organizational theory, and other clusters of knowledge are relevant for social work if they are appropriately integrated with its purpose and focus. If used separately, however, they tend to pull the practitioner away from the social work focus toward that of the other profession or discipline from which they are derived, as Coyle pointed out. Social workers have often tended to identify

---

[18] Grace Longwell Coyle, *Social Science in the Professional Education of Social Workers* (New York: Council on Social Work Education, 1958), pp. 12–13.

[19] *Ibid.*

with psychiatrists, social scientists, or others, rather than to move their knowledge fully over into social work's own area of practice. The kind of integrative thinking that would fit social work's concern, that would bring together the person and his environment, eluded capture for a long time. Late in the midcentury a change in social work thinking began to appear. This is illustrated in the gradual evolution of a body of knowledge regarding the successive stages in human growth and development originally developed for teaching courses on human behavior in schools of social work. From a single focus on the psychic aspects of personality, knowledge has been expanded to show the individual within his culture and his society with its institutions. Erikson's contribution regarding the healthy personality, ego identity, and the psychosocial crises of growth has been a major addition.[20] For a considerable period, the biological and intellectual components of growth received little attention; now they are being given greater recognition.

Knowledge Derived from Social Work Experience

Prior to the 1950s, since social workers possessed only limited bodies of theory, they were necessarily practicing to a large degree on the basis of commonsense principles and their own developing experience in helping people with various kinds of psychosocial problems. With increasing awareness of their responsibility to develop their own knowledge, social workers began to turn their attention to this practice experience as a source. Might it be that social work has special opportunities for developing a distinctive body of knowledge?

In their role as members of a helping profession, many social workers (the majority of the profession) are working directly with the people they serve. They seek to assess the impact of the situation upon the people involved in it and to understand its particular meaning to them, that is, their perception, feelings, and desires in regard to it. In accordance with this approach, the relationship established with the persons being helped and the

---

20 Erik H. Erikson, "Identity and the Life Cycle," in George S. Klein, ed., *Psychological Issues* (New York: International Universities Press, 1959), pp. 18–171.

interviewing method aim to enable people to talk freely about their problems and life goals. As social workers observe and listen in this way and intervene in an effort to bring about change, they feel the emotional stress themselves and through this sharing sense vividly the significance of the situation in human terms. Thus through their closeness to a wide range of social problems, their way of relating to people, and their participation in the living experience, social workers have special opportunities for understanding problems of social functioning.

This second major source of social work knowledge—the experience of professionals in working with people and helping them to meet a wide range of life problems—is generally described as "practice wisdom" and most of it is submerged in practice. It has not been formulated and, therefore, its extent is unrecognized and its importance underestimated. Some of it can be extracted from the social work literature but it has not been codified and so is not readily available for use. But by far the greater part of practice knowledge is imbedded in practice. It is taught and used as part of one of the methods—casework, group work, or community organization. It is passed on from one social worker to another through supervision and conferences. Here the method-and-skill model of social work practice, which emphasized the art, has stimulated the development of knowledge within the methods but has not favored the development of systematized knowledge for the profession as a whole. In the concern with "feeling" and "doing," what is "known" too often is not even identified as knowledge or expressed as knowledge generalizations. This is serious because there is a real possibility that some of what social work has learned and is continually learning may not become known to other professions and disciplines or to society, all of whom might use it to improve social welfare. One committee of the National Association of Social Workers that was examining the problem of building social work knowledge stressed particularly the importance of capturing and articulating what is known by practitioners but has not been sufficiently verbalized or communicated to the field at large and is not yet recognized substantively as part of social work's body of knowledge.[21]

---

[21] *Building Social Work Knowledge: Report of a Conference*, p. 111.

In recent years, preliminary efforts to get at the practitioner's knowledge (not reported in the literature) indicate that the process of lifting it out of practice will not be easy. Although admittedly this understanding and these insights must dwell in the practitioner, since they contribute to his skill, he seems unready to recognize and formulate what he knows. What questions, then, can be asked of him? How can he be helped to identify and articulate what he is learning from his direct experience in working with people?

Such knowledge embedded in practice can be illustrated by a paper on factors in treatment written by Towle in the thirties. The client, she said, "may gain increased self-understanding and self-acceptance with a resultant increased capacity for solving his difficulties through the treatment interview in which he is helped to secure release of feeling and in which he experiences acceptance of that feeling." And again, the caseworker "grants him the reality of his feeling about his problem so that in the process of revealing his needs he may experience help, which may lead him to seek further assistance in other areas." [22] Her paper is focused on casework treatment, but one senses that underneath the discussion of method lie some generalizations about giving and receiving help that have broader relevance than for casework treatment alone.

At another point Towle suggests a number of criteria for determining the "treatment possibilities in a case." Among these are the duration of the symptomatic behavior, the extent of the life experience involved, and the mobility of the environment.[23] These factors are obviously relevant for understanding the efforts of individuals to deal with their life problems. Such generalizations do not, however, take their place as part of the profession's knowledge until they get lifted out of the "treatment" context and are formulated as knowledge about social behavior. This is seen in the fact that Towle's criteria were not taken up and widely used later in practice and teaching, as they would have been if their full implications had been realized.

Once alerted to the matter of submerged social work knowl-

---

[22] Towle, *op. cit.*, pp. 319 and 321.
[23] *Ibid.*, pp. 322–325.

edge, one can find recurrent instances when examining the literature. A discussion of unconscious collusion in marital interaction suggests the significance of social workers' experience in this area; but the paper concentrates on the handling of two cases and in its conclusion emphasizes the casework treatment (i.e., the method), so that the knowledge generalizations do not emerge.[24] A paper on counseling with parents of retarded children living at home emphasizes the ever present ambivalence of the parents and their guilt feelings, which are enhanced by the fact that they cannot rationally project any responsibility or blame for the problem on the child himself. The essential knowledge is clearly brought out but subordinated to the emphasis on counseling (i.e., the method).[25] It is evident that social workers need and are ready to move beyond the traditional discussion of skill and process toward the formulation of social work knowledge about the problems in which they are intervening. These formulations should be in the form of distinctly social work propositions and generalizations, in other words, relating to the behavior of people under stress, the meaning of the situation to them, their efforts at coping, their ways of seeking and using help, and similar phenomena, all of which fall within the particular experience of social work.

What is becoming evident is that social work does not yet possess all the necessary intellectual approaches and tools for building its knowledge, whether through selecting it from outside sources or extracting it from its own experience. Some years ago when sociology faced this same problem, Blumer pointed out that at an early stage of growth a discipline or profession develops a wide range of "sensitizing concepts," which can be expected eventually to come together into some central themes.[26] It is possible, however, that in social work it is difficult to bring such scattered concepts together because it is taking such a long time to develop a frame of reference. This is particularly true if the members of

---

[24] Barbara Gray Ellis, "Unconscious Collusion in Marital Interaction," *Social Casework,* Vol. 45, No. 2 (February 1964), pp. 79–85.

[25] Sylvia Schild, "Counseling with Parents of Retarded Children Living at Home," *Social Work,* Vol. 9, No. 1 (January 1964), pp. 86–91.

[26] Herbert Blumer, "What Is Wrong with Social Theory?" *American Sociological Review,* Vol. 19, No. 1 (February 1954), pp. 3–10.

the profession do not accept their responsibility for the necessary kind of integrative thinking. For instance, even though research techniques have been taught to social work students for decades, social work has been slow to develop its own basic research, an essential activity of any mature profession.

Thus efforts toward knowledge-building show clearly the urgent need for a common perspective in the profession—a perspective broad enough not to have a constricting influence on new thinking and yet focused enough to provide sufficient convergence to permit cumulative thinking. In spite of the limitations in the current situation, there is encouragement in the probability that more knowledge is at hand than has been realized and in the intent to move toward more deliberate building of the profession's knowledge.

Social Work Intervention

The second subcommittee on the Working Definition found that the notion of method presented greater difficulties than value and knowledge. The idea of method in social work seems to have become inextricably tied up with a whole mode of approach and for many social workers encompasses the relevant knowledge and values as well as the techniques. Since social work method is thus not defined or definable in its usual sense as systematic procedure, the committee used another concept to describe the professional act. *"Professional intervention,"* they said, "is used to refer to the action of the practitioner which is directed to some part of a social system or process with the intention of inducing a change in it." [27] Such a professional act is guided and carried out through the conscious use of social work knowledge and values and thus is consonant with the idea of their priority. The choice of "intervention" was deliberate, since intervention traditionally means making a difference in outcome or course of events.

The older notion of method developed within the method-and-skill model when the art of social work was emphasized. Each individual social worker was expected to leave the school of social

[27] Gordon, "A Critique of the Working Definition," pp. 10–11.

work with skill in one method that would prepare him for beginning practice in an agency.[28] As attention was directed to the examination of practice in the fifties and sixties, however, it became evident that the notion of a social worker prepared to use a single method no longer conformed with the changing picture.[29] "Caseworkers" were working with groups and "group workers" with individuals. In fact, the traditional three methods were now found to cover only a portion of the professional social worker's action. Growing numbers of social workers were acting as consultants and others were developing new approaches in the area of social policy and social planning.

The idea of social work intervention was increasingly used by practitioners and began to appear in the literature. When the concept was explored by the NASW Commission on Practice in 1966, a review of the literature revealed that it was used with varied meanings.[30] It was already proving useful, however, in offering a broader view than the traditional concept of method. The idea developed that, although selected methods and techniques may at any one time be emphasized in a particular area of practice, the full "interventive repertoire" is potentially relevant and applicable to any field of practice.[31] Thus the possibility of a wide range of interventive acts and the responsibility for selecting among them in relation to their pertinence for various situations was opened up to the profession. This was a significant advance in thinking, which demonstrates how ideas and concepts can either impede or facilitate a profession's ability to master its practice.

In viewing intervention at the level of the entire profession's

---

[28] Ruth E. Smalley, *Specialization in Social Work Education* (New York: Council on Social Work Education, 1956), p. 5.

[29] Helen Harris Perlman, "Social Work Method: A Review of the Past Decade," *Trends in Social Work Practice and Knowledge: NASW Tenth Anniversary Symposium* (New York: National Association of Social Workers, 1966), pp. 79–96.

[30] Max Bogner, "The Concept of Intervention in Social Work," a working paper prepared for the Commission on Practice (New York: National Association of Social Workers, 1966). (Mimeographed.)

[31] Genevieve W. Carter, *Fields of Practice: Report of a Workshop* (New York: National Association of Social Workers, 1965).

practice, the question might arise as to why such a comprehensive concept did not develop before. Why did social work thinking crystallize around the three methods? The movement beyond case-work toward the development of group work and community organization was important in widening the scope of the profession's practice. It demonstrated social workers' intent to develop competence in working with groups and communities as well as individuals and families, thus laying out a broad role in society before most other helping professions began to think in these terms. The three methods, however, could not easily be extended to encompass the rapidly expanding practice. New interventive approaches, such as consultation and social planning, found no place within them. Furthermore, as time went on and social workers trained in one method were actually using much from each other's methods in working with individuals, groups, and communities, the pattern of skill in a single social work method no longer fitted the changing situation.

The notion of intervention has made possible a comprehensive view of social work practice. Like all new ideas that are being explored, the important point is not whether a special term or word is eventually used but the gain that comes from an idea broad and flexible enough to move thinking along in new directions. We propose now to take the concept of the interventive repertoire and use it within the framework of the Working Definition instead of the concept of method.

It should be clear that value and knowledge are not a part of intervention but are separate entities. *Interventive* acts and techniques are means to an end and are only significant when the end is defined in terms of social work purposes and values and the situation is accurately understood through the use of social work knowledge. *It is through the conscious action of the social worker, who selects what is relevant for the particular situation before him, that the appropriate knowledge and values become integrated with the intervention.* The implication of this analysis will be discussed in subsequent chapters. Meanwhile, the dependence of intervention upon knowledge and value should be continually kept in mind.[32]

---

[32] *See* Ruth Elizabeth Smalley, *Theory for Social Work Practice* (New York: Columbia University Press, 1967). In contrast to the viewpoint

The interventive repertoire is conceived as covering multiple interventive measures and techniques, in fact, all that social work is using at any one time. Concentration on a few methods has tended to direct attention away from the richness and variety of the profession's potential contribution, since some of these measures have received little attention in the professional literature or curriculum. A number of promising approaches, developed in specific sections of practice, remained almost unknown to the profession as a whole. Consultation has already been mentioned as one example. The capacity to view its full potential is important for social work at this time of broad social change when flexibility and choice among alternatives become necessary and often urgent. There is then not only a greater recognition of unrealized capacities but also more chance of evolving interventive measures in response to new needs. Viewed this way, social work's interventive measures range from the helping service given an individual by one social worker to the widest efforts to influence change in social conditions affecting large population groups.

The professional relationship with the client is viewed by many social workers as the central channel for giving help. The concept of the casework relationship, however, has been so interwoven with knowledge, value, and method that clear distinctions have not been made. On the other hand, some of social work's other important concepts, such as acceptance of the client and self-awareness by the worker, have been furthered by the idea of the professional relationship as developed by social workers. Obviously, the concept of relationship has been both a strength and a problem in its influence on the profession's growth.

In the perception of interventive action, so-called direct and indirect service—working with clients and with others—have usually been regarded as separate and as being carried on by different practitioners, such as "caseworkers" and "community organizers." One must look at the full interventive repertoire in order to become aware of its scope and the interdependence of the various interventive approaches. Since for a considerable period certain interventive measures, described as methods, were perceived as

presented here, which views intervention as being dependent on and growing out of knowledge and values, Smalley presents "generic principles of social work method" as basic for social work practice.

primary, other activities were carried on informally and were not recognized as significant professional techniques. For instance, it was accepted that agency administrators or executives used the administrative method, but it was not realized that experienced staff workers were also involved in many less conspicuous actions that, taken together, could have important impact on procedures and even on social policy in the agency or program. Admission policies in medical institutions and eligibility procedures in public welfare agencies were influenced in this way. Social workers were also observed conferring with their professional colleagues—such as nurses, teachers, physicians, and correctional officers—but that this could be regarded as professional consultation was not realized until social workers began to be employed in positions in which they were described as consultants. It now seems possible that some of these less recognized activities will in future become more potent in influencing social change than those that were traditionally emphasized.[33]

The trend appears to be toward a time when all social workers will need to be able to view the full interventive repertoire of the profession and to understand how the various interventive actions are combined and used in practice. It is not a matter of acquiring skill. It does not mean that practitioners must acquire competence in all the techniques; that would be an impossible achievement. It means that all social workers will be aware of the full range of interventive measures encompassed by their profession, not as skills to be learned but as ways of offering help, influencing situations, and bringing about social change, and will take them into account in their own planning and action.

Bringing the Essential Elements Together

The Working Definition states that certain elements must be present in all practice, at least to some degree, if it is to be re-

---

[33] Harriett M. Bartlett, "The Widening Scope of Hospital Social Work," *Social Casework*, Vol. 44, No. 1 (January 1963), pp. 3–10; and Bartlett, "An Approach for Analyzing Any Field of Social Work Practice," *Social Work Activities in Public Health* (Boston: Massachusetts Department of Public Health, 1962), pp. 33–41.

garded as social work practice.[34] These are here defined as knowledge, value, and the interventive repertoire, which are considered the *essential elements* in social work practice. The effort to identify the essential elements helps us to perceive the profession from a new perspective. When the method-and-skill model in the earlier days focused upon the individual practitioner and his incorporation of the necessary attitudes, knowledge, and techniques, concentration at this level of practice blocked interest and progress in building up bodies of values and knowledge. In one sense, it would seem that the point at which the practitioner delivers the service would be the one that should have logical priority and emphasis. This is what many social workers asserted and explains the long-continued emphases on skill and the professional relationship. However, if we look at the full picture, we see that in order to operate in society, professions must have available a growing body of concepts, generalizations, and theory in the form of abstract propositions for the education of their students and the use of their practitioners.

These ideas are put together in the form of a diagram on page 82. Although apparently simple, the diagram illustrates a number of important points, as follows:

1. It enables us to perceive social work practice as a whole.

2. It shows the essential elements as visible bodies of values, knowledge, and interventive measures. They are no longer submerged in or divided among separate methods.

3. It shows the priority of knowledge and value.

4. It recognizes that what is learned from the profession's own experience (the interventive action of practitioners) feeds back into the profession's bodies of knowledge and values, continually enriching them.

The essential elements appear as bodies of abstract values, knowledge and theory, and interventive measures. It is these values and this knowledge that guide practitioners and it is through these interventive measures that practitioners influence situations with which they are concerned. When professions are compared, it can be seen that each has its own particular combination of values,

---

[34] *See* "Working Definition of Social Work Practice" in the Appendix, p. 221.

FIGURE 1. SOCIAL WORK PRACTICE

Essential Elements

in

Social Work Practice

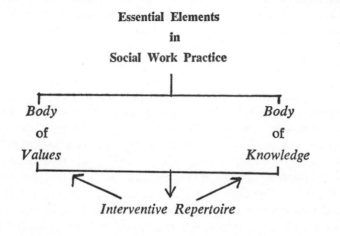

Interventive Repertoire

---

knowledge, and techniques. In all established professions, a considerable amount of agreement exists regarding these basic elements, which are taught in the schools and applied in practice. They are the source of the profession's strength and distinctiveness.

Some people object to the description of knowledge and values as separate elements because they so obviously permeate all social work practice. However, since our examination of social workers' perceptions of their practice shows that the development of the profession has been retarded by the failure of its members to recognize the importance of these basic components of a profession, distinguish between them, and apply them consciously in practice, it becomes important and appropriate to use concepts that will permit such distinctions to be made. It is necessary to understand the nature of professional values and knowledge as entities and their relationship to each other in order to know how to organize and develop them for professional use.

Many social workers have difficulty in visualizing such a general concept of the profession or in perceiving why it is important. Actually, it is of immediate and practical importance because, when the helping service of the individual practitioner is placed within the overall *professional* model and his activity rests on a body of common social work values and knowledge developed within this framework, the whole scene shifts. The practitioner is no longer conceived as a worker who is primarily skilled in one method. He now becomes a *social worker,* broadly gauged, who develops competence in all the essentials of the profession. He leaves the school with an initial grasp of social work's full scope and content. After some years of practice he develops into a competent social worker, whose practice is soundly and securely based on the common elements in his profession. In placing the practice of the individual practitioner within the professional model, as we have done in this chapter, we eliminate the dysjunction that existed in the past when individual practice was based on skill and method rather than the value-knowledge-intervention base of the profession.

In the opening chapter we listed some steps in thinking that must be taken by the profession in order to meet its responsibilities in society today. Several of these—particularly the view of social work practice as a whole, identification of the common elements, and recognition of barriers to integrative thinking—have been dealt with up to this point in the discussion of the practice models, the method-and-skill model and the professional model. The professional model for practice has, however, been discussed only in its general outlines. We shall now move into a consideration of some of social work's important characteristics—especially its central focus and knowledge—in order to give more substance and meaning to our propositions.

6

focus on

social functioning

Members of a profession that encompasses so many wide-ranging interests as social work should consider whether there are some central themes that will help them bring their interests together. In a federal government office a social worker is serving as a member of a national advisory committee to develop policy recommendations regarding basic problems of public welfare. In a storefront office in an urban ghetto a social worker is planning a program to get urgently needed services to the deprived residents of the crowded neighborhood. On a street corner in another city a social worker is getting to know a group of adolescent youths, composed largely of dropouts, whom he hopes to guide to a project for job training. Going out into a community from a mental health center, a social worker is giving consultation to schools, courts, and welfare agencies regarding the intricate problems of human behavior with which they must deal. In a room in a children's agency a social worker sits with one small frightened child who was left alone in his home by his mother's sudden death and whose future life he must now begin to plan. Is it possible to find a comprehensive concept to cover such situations that, at first glance, appear to vary so widely in nature and scope? This chapter will examine the development of such a concept and its potential as an integrative concept for social work.

The problems and phenomena with which social work is concerned are not easily distinguished and defined. How does one separate family problems from children's problems and both in turn from health and housing problems? Such problems are widespread and diffuse because they run all through life. They are so intertwined with life situations that they resist recognition and identification as separate entities. They involve complex biopsychosocial interactions in which the critical elements are not readily defined. Their constant modification through rapid social change increases the difficulty—and also the urgency—of dealing with them. Finally, because concern about social problems is shared so widely with other professionals, legislators, and citizens, many of whom believe they can deal with these problems themselves, it is not easy for a profession like social work to identify its peculiar area of interest and competence.

However, the complexity and elusiveness of the problem do not seem to explain fully why an easily recognized central focus has not emerged in social work as it has in so many other professions. One explanation for this lag is to be found in the way social workers think and operate, as described earlier, which has produced fragmentation in practice and unintended barriers against moving to a common focus for the entire profession.

Identifying a Profession's Focus

In our earlier analysis of social workers' thinking about their practice, we found that they were primarily interested in helping as an *activity* and worked intensively to define the processes involved and the skills required for effective helping. This applied to the full range of work, whether with individuals, groups, or communities. Ideas regarding the problems and situations to be dealt with were tied in with and subordinated to the processes and methods. Therefore, throughout its history, social work has had no generally accepted, comprehensive concept to describe and identify its area of central concern as a profession.

It is the thesis of this discussion that a profession like social work, whose members must be able to deal with intricate social situations, cannot—and will not—attain its full strength and become a fully functioning profession until its members can identify their area of central concern and define the nature of the problems, situations, and social phenomena with which their helping process and professional actions are concerned. Further, change and complexity in the area of social relationships today make it harder for social work to do this than other professions that deal with older and more easily understood areas of human need or function, such as health, education, and law.

The helping process in social work, which demands the capacity to influence social behavior and social conditions, depends upon adequate understanding of their nature. The practitioner must command and use relevant knowledge. The building of such a body of professional knowledge requires identification of the particular phenomena with which the profession deals and concepts for organizing thinking regarding these phenomena. For a profession like social work to be effective in today's society, it must identify an area of central concern that is (1) common to the profession as a whole, (2) meaningful in terms of the profession's values and goals, (3) practical in terms of available and attainable knowledge and techniques, and (4) sufficiently distinctive so that it does not duplicate what other professions are doing. To do this demands readiness to work as intensively on understanding social phenomena and social situations as on understanding processes, methods, and action. It calls for the kind of integrative thinking that will draw from social work's past the ideas that are relevant, combine them with new ideas, and build the essential components into powerful, comprehensive concepts regarding the profession's focus, which will demonstrate convincingly to its members and to society where the profession stands and what it has to offer.

Early Concepts

If asked to describe their profession, most social workers would probably emphasize two central ideas: (1) it is a helping profession and (2) it is concerned with the social functioning of people. What is meant by the notion of a helping profession? It is a profession that brings services to people, with the aim of modifying situations to improve the welfare of individuals and society. Thus it is change oriented. Since change involves doing something about a situation, the professional worker is a participant in the change process. The social worker who helps a client change his attitudes or a group of agencies to co-ordinate their services is necessarily a part of the situation as long as the change process is going on. Each service profession gives special meaning to the idea of helping according to its own perspective, particularly its values and ways of working with people.

What, then, is added by the notion that social workers offer help in the area of social functioning? Obviously no one profession can claim this as its exclusive domain because it is too broad. Understandably, others are already moving in to stake their claim. If the idea of social functioning is to be used as a starting point, it must be defined further. As now used in social work, the idea is too vague and is being used with too many varied meanings.

Throughout most of its history, social work has had no central concept to describe its area of responsibility and expertise. Some social workers have stressed their concern with social problems, others with the skilled process. Still others have concentrated on a particular field of practice, such as family welfare, health, or corrections. In spite of these apparently varied interests, certain consistent and cumulative trends in thinking can be traced.

In earlier days social workers were concerned equally with problems of individuals and population groups. One interest took the form of social casework and the other resembled what is now called "social action." Although the thirties and forties showed a marked swing toward service to individuals, the interest in broader social conditions and problems calling for social work's concern was never lost and reappeared strongly toward the midcentury, restoring the old balance. Furthermore, in their literature, practice, and teaching, social workers characteristically perceived the individual as a person functioning in a social situation. Even though the concepts developed in social casework centered on personality, social workers never gave up their concern for the environment and its impact on the individual. The term "psychosocial" was increasingly used to describe the social work focus.[1]

---

[1] See the following references in Cora Kasius, ed., *Social Casework in the Fifties* (New York: Family Service Association of America, 1962):

Certainly it may be said that for a considerable period interest centered on the psychic aspects, the significance of the social environment was devalued, and a serious effort to bring the "psychic" and the "social" together was not made. Yet in spite of its ambivalence, the young profession persisted in asserting its continuous interest in both the person and his environment and recognizing that to fullfill its purpose as a helping profession it must eventually come to grips with the whole person-in-situation phenomenon, in all its facets and with all its implications.

Regrettably, early efforts at such conceptualization were not picked up and used. In her discussion of social evidence, Richmond placed the client in his family and neighborhood and suggested the key questions relevant to a number of typical social situations, such as the immigrant family and the widow with children.[2] This part of her thinking, however, was lost to casework teaching and theory when psychotherapy claimed primary interest.

In 1935 Cannon presented an interpretation of the social work focus that is equally relevant more than thirty years later. She said:

No longer in the mind of the social case worker is poverty a sort of moral failure or even a disease of personality; it is a discrepancy between individual capacity and environmental demand upon it. No longer is rehabilitation of the dependent the social case worker's concept of cure, but rather the restoration of balance by strengthening environmental support on the one hand and releasing resident energies in the individual on the other.[3]

In 1937 Sheffield suggested that the unit with which social casework deals should be the "need situation," as defined by a "so-

---

Gordon Hamilton, "The Role of Social Casework in Social Policy," pp. 33 and 43, and Samuel Finestone, "The Scientific Component in the Casework Field Curriculum," pp. 315–320. *See also* Isabel L. Stamm, "Ego Psychology in the Emerging Theoretical Base of Casework," in Alfred J. Kahn, ed., *Issues in American Social Work* (New York: Columbia University Press, 1958), pp. 84–87.

[2] Mary E. Richmond, *Social Diagnosis* (New York: Russell Sage Foundation, 1917).

[3] M. Antoinette Cannon, "Where the Changes in Social Case Work Have Brought Us," in Fern Lowry, ed., *Readings in Social Case Work: 1920–1938* (New York: Columbia University Press, 1939), p. 112.

cially developing purpose." [4]   Thus the concepts of *environment* and *situation* keep appearing in the literature.

In 1946 Pray carried on with the theme. Social work comes into play, he said, when familiar, satisfying social relationships are threatened, weakened, and broken and when people seek help in finding more meaningful relationships or in replenishing their strength for meeting the difficulties and "realizing the potentialities of their social situations." Other professions are also interested in the individual but, unlike the others, social work is never primarily concerned with the separate, inner personal life but always with the individual in his social relationships.[5] By this time there was greater readiness for such thinking and Pray's formulation was widely used.

In 1951 Hamilton, on the opening page of her well-known text on social casework, spoke of two nuclear ideas that distinguish social work as one of the humanistic professions. "The first," she said, "is that the human event consists of person and situation, or subjective and objective reality, which constantly interact." [6] This idea of person and situation interacting is elaborated throughout her book.

In 1958 the Working Definition described the practitioner's concern with the interaction between the individual and the social environment but did not develop the concept further. It was Boehm who, in discussing the nature of social work, formally presented the concept of social functioning, which was being used at that time, and clarified its meaning by relating it to social interaction. The primary focus of social work is on social interaction, he pointed out. The individual and his environment should not be viewed as two separate entities but as an interactional field. In explaning this further, he said:

The nature of any problem in the area of social interaction is determined both by the individual's potential capacity for

---

[4] Ada Eliot Sheffield, *Social Insight in Case Situations* (New York: D. Appleton-Century Co., 1937), pp. 96–97.

[5] Kenneth L. M. Pray, *Social Work in a Revolutionary Age* (Philadelphia: University of Pennsylvania Press, 1949), pp. 236–237.

[6] Gordon Hamilton, *Theory and Practice of Social Case Work* (New York: Columbia University Press, 1951), p. 3.

relationships in performance of his social roles and by the social resources he uses to satisfy his needs for self-fulfillment. Hence, the social worker focuses at one and the same time upon the capacity of individuals and groups for effective interaction and upon social resources from the point of view of their contribution to effective social functioning. In the light of this dual focus the social worker initiates (alone or with related professional or nonprofessional community groups) steps (1) to increase the effectiveness of individuals' interaction with each other, singly, and in groups; and (2) to mobilize appropriate social resources by coordinating, changing, or creating them anew.[7]

Boehm's interpretation was first published concurrently with the Working Definition and later included in the Social Work Curriculum Study of the Council on Social Work Education in 1959.[8] His interpretation of social functioning in terms of role performance, a conceptual approach used by many social workers, is not pursued in this discussion because other concepts that appeared later seem more promising for social work.

An Example from One Field

Meanwhile other streams of thinking—not recognized as significant at the time—were gathering and flowing together. One of these began in one of the oldest fields of practice, medical social work. Early in this century social workers were drawn into hospitals and clinics by socially minded physicians. This field of practice was based upon a large scientific body of knowledge, centering around the reality problems of illness and medical care, which have a sharp disruptive impact on individuals and families. The physicians, accustomed to scientific thinking and orderly processes in dealing with patients, encouraged social workers to examine and clarify their own practice. A pioneer study, published when medi-

---

[7] Werner W. Boehm, *Objectives of the Social Work Curriculum of the Future* (New York: Council on Social Work Education, 1959), pp. 47–48.
[8] *See* Werner W. Boehm, "The Nature of Social Work," *Social Work,* Vol. 3, No. 2 (April 1958), pp. 10–18; and *ibid.*

cal social work was just fifteen years old, was significant because it began with the central phenomenon—that of illness—and described it from a social work viewpoint. In this study and one that followed later, Thornton identified the hospital social worker's concern as those "social conditions which bear directly on the health of the patient, either inducing susceptibility to ill-health, or helping or hindering the securing and completing of medical care." [9] Social problems created by the illness for other members of the family were also included. This concept, which was later defined as the *social component in illness and medical care,* encompassed factors in the personality as well as the environment. Thus from the beginning there was recognition of social workers' responsibility to apply their own thinking to their area of practice and to conceptualize the central problem in social work terms.

As psychiatric thinking spread through social work and psychosomatic medicine developed, the term "social component" was less used, but the basic concept persisted. At this stage *the meaning of illness to the patient and family* was particularly emphasized. Beginning in the thirties, a considerable literature dealing with the psychosocial aspects of illness developed. In these discussions, social workers clearly identified with the patients and families and endeavored to understand the impact of illness on them, their feelings about it, their difficulties with medical care, and their responses to the situation. The concepts of stress in psychosomatic medicine, prevention in public health, and disability in rehabilitation, all contributed to this thinking.[10]

By the early fifties considerable progress had been made. Starting from the original concept of disease, social workers had moved a long way toward a concept of the psychosocial implications of

---

[9] *The Functions of Hospital Social Service* (Chicago: American Association of Hospital Social Workers, 1930), p. 59; and Janet Thornton, *The Social Component in Medical Care* (New York: Columbia University Press, 1937).

[10] Some representative papers are Irene Grant, "Social Work with Tuberculous Patients," *The Family,* Vol. 13, No. 6 (October 1932), pp. 190–197; Ethel Cohen, "The Social Component in Heart Disease," *American Heart Journal,* Vol. 16, No. 4 (October 1938), pp. 422–430; Alice A. Grant, "Medical Social Work in an Epidemic of Poliomyelitis," *Journal of Pediatrics,* Vol. 24, No. 6 (June 1944), pp. 691–723; and Caroline H. Elledge, "The Meaning of Illness," *Medical Social Work,* Vol. 2, No. 2 (April 1953), pp. 49–65.

illness as perceived by social work. There were factors in the situation, however, that were limiting further progress. In working on the various medical services in the hospital, social workers became familiar with one or another medical condition, observed the psychosocial problems presented to patients, and set out to describe them. Working in continuous collaboration with physicians as they did, it was natural to start from the medical condition. After a while, however, it began to appear that some of the problems described as characteristic of one condition were also found to be associated with other conditions. There was increasing overlapping and duplication of ideas. What was happening was that social workers, writing about medical problems in this way, were still under the influence of the medical frame of reference. It was pointed out in Chapter 2 that social work was growing through its fields. Here it seemed that the growth had gone as far as possible within the field. How then could the necessary steps be taken to break through and move clearly into a social work frame of reference?

If we re-examine this stream of thinking about the psychosocial aspects of illness, we can see that it was steadily moving toward a concept of social functioning as related to illness. But a social work concept was needed that could be applied to any field. When the medical social workers found themselves hemmed in within the medical frame of reference, the idea of social functioning was still too vague to be useful. Nevertheless, some progress toward such a concept was made. These social workers had not allowed themselves to be confined by "casework," "skill," and "setting," but had used a broader social work approach for understanding and describing the problems regarded as central to their practice. Their ideas encompassed both the personality and the environment. There was continuous concern for both the emotional aspects and the socioeconomic impact of illness on individuals and families.

In seeking to analyze and describe the problems presented to patients and their families by illness and medical care, social workers began to recognize recurrent experiences—such as mutilation of the body, physical helplessness, uncertainty of outlook, and fear of death—which present difficulties for all persons who must go through them. Thus there began to be movement away from concentration on specific diseases (the medical approach) or on unique reactions of individuals (the casework approach) toward identification of *common* psychosocial problems of illness viewed within a social work perspective.

Emerging Social Work Concepts

The next step—to move from the confines of one particular field of practice toward the definition and use of basic social work concepts in any field of practice—has been facilitated by two directions of thinking that were stimulating to social workers. One was the conceptualization of human growth and development as the successive mastery of the particular problems presented to the individual by each new life cycle through which he passes. The second was the crisis concept, first formulated in mental health and further developed by social workers and behavioral scientists. Here the problems presented by crucial life situations—whether the life cycles of individual growth or specific traumatic episodes like illness—are conceived as tasks that must be met and dealt with in some way. The aspect with which social workers are most concerned is repeatedly described as the coping efforts of people to deal with these tasks. A related concern is the consequences of crisis for people in terms of their opportunity for further growth.[11] In examining these converging ideas further, we should have in mind the requirements for such concepts, if they are to identify the focus of the profession. They should have high relevance and applicability to the essential elements of social work, particularly its values. They should concentrate on a few related phenomena to avoid diffuseness and yet be general enough to cover the range of phenomena found in social work practice. They should have theoretical interest so that they can stimulate research and be tested. They should move social work thinking toward greater integration.[12]

---

[11] Ruth M. Butler, *An Orientation to Knowledge of Human Growth and Behavior in Social Work Education* (New York: Council on Social Work Education, 1959); and Howard J. Parad, ed., *Crisis Intervention: Selected Readings* (New York: Family Service Association of America, 1965).

[12] William E. Gordon, "Knowledge and Value: Their Distinction and Relationship in Clarifying Social Work Practice," *Social Work,* Vol. 10, No. 3 (July 1965), pp. 32–39.

It should be clear that we are not concerned here with method or intervention, agency programs, or the field of social welfare. These are, of course, all related matters. But we are at this point concentrating on the effort to identify social work's central focus— the problems, situations, and phenomena with which it is primarily concerned.

The Concept of Task

Taking the ideas that had been emerging from social work, we shall see how, used in combination with concepts from other professions, they led toward an integrative concept. The concept of life tasks is one of these.[13] As has been shown, the idea that there are situations which present problems to groups of people and must be dealt with by them in some way began to develop rather early in social work. This was implicit in the concept of "the social component in illness" as developed in medical social work. In 1940 the writer, in discussing the meaning of illness to the patient, described "recurrent situations in illness or medical care that are difficult for many patients," such as entering the hospital or having some part of the body removed, and the manner in which the problem is revealed through the patient's difficulty in taking the necessary step in relation to his medical care.[14] Social workers in other fields were exploring similar ideas, such as the meaning of money, family breakdown, and marital friction. They were not, however, able to move toward the kind of general concept needed for social work because of their concentration on the uniqueness of the individual and emotional aspects of behavior. It was the psychiatrists, because they also individualized patients but through their scientific medical training were accustomed to generalize, who pointed the way. Men like Lindemann and Bowlby recognized that there were life situations, such as bereavement and separation, which presented problems to most people, and that

---

[13] In the social work literature the task concept is also used to refer to the professional task of the social worker. Here it is used only in relation to the people who are coping with life problems.

[14] Harriett M. Bartlett, *Some Aspects of Social Casework in a Medical Setting* (Chicago: American Association of Social Workers, 1940), pp. 117 and 123.

these situations could be described as psychosocial phenomena.[15] In his discussion of ego identity, Erikson described what he called "psychosocial crises" at each maturational stage.[16]

It is not clear when the term "task" first came to be used in social work. Writers in psychiatry used such terms as "syndrome" and "crisis." Rapoport, a psychologist, in a study of the critical transition points in the normal family life cycle, such as getting married, described the "inherent tasks" and related them to the coping process.[17] Austin, a social worker, also brought together the ideas of tasks and coping.[18]

The crisis model was originally developed in the mental health field and was concerned with prevention of mental disorders. It directed attention primarily to emotional disturbances and psychological problems.[19] At first, social workers tended to follow this lead, with an emphasis on ego psychology. They also discussed the task-crisis concept in terms of their customary methods framework and wrote about "short-term casework," "preventive casework," and "crisis intervention."[20] However, to develop the task concept effectively within a social work framework requires some shift in emphasis. Tasks refer to social phenomena, not techniques. The task is a way of describing critical and demanding situations that confront people. Social workers must be equally concerned with the psychic and social implications of situations for the functioning of people in their social relationships

---

[15] Erich Lindemann, "Symptomatology and Management of Acute Grief," in Parad, ed., op. cit., pp. 7–21; and John Bowlby, Maternal Care and Mental Health (Geneva, Switzerland: World Health Organization, 1951).

[16] Erik H. Erikson, "The Problem of Ego Identity," in George S. Klein, ed., Psychological Issues (New York: International Universities Press, 1950), p. 166.

[17] Rhona Rapoport, "Normal Crises, Family Structure, and Mental Health," in Parad, ed., op. cit., pp. 75–87.

[18] Lucille N. Austin, Foreword, in Parad, ed., op. cit., p. xii.

[19] See Gerald Caplan, "General Introduction and Overview," pp. 8–10, and Donald C. Klein and Erich Lindemann, "Preventive Intervention in Individual and Family Crisis Situations," pp. 283–305, in Caplan, ed., Prevention of Mental Disorders in Children (New York: Basic Books, 1961).

[20] Parad, op. cit.

—which is a somewhat different approach from that of psychia-trists.[21]

As used in social work, the task concept is a way of describing the demands made upon people by various life situations. These have to do with daily living, such as growing up in the family, learning in school, entering the world of work, marrying and rear-ing a family, and also with the common traumatic situations of life such as bereavement, separation, illness, or financial difficulties. These tasks call for responses in the form of attitude or action from the people involved in the situation. They are common problems that confront many (or all) people. The responses may differ but most people must deal with the problems in some way or other. Thus progress in identifying the characteristics of such tasks will lead to better understanding of the problems that people face in their daily living.

The task concept is not a comprehensive theory like Erikson's theory of human maturation but a single concept referring to one aspect of psychosocial behavior with which social workers are concerned. Thinking about tasks leads to such questions as: What are the tasks presented to individuals and families in meeting the shock of serious illness, the attendant anxiety, and the perma-nent physical handicap that frequently results? [22] What task faces the delinquent in prison if he is to move from the restricted prison environment toward a responsible role in community life? Some-times the steps to be taken in dealing with tasks are sequential, in that later steps depend on earlier ones. For example, the child must accept separation from home in order to attend school. The adult must give up the protection of the hospital or prison in order to carry family responsibilities.

Since the task concept directs attention to common problems and life situations that many people face, it cuts across old bar-riers which fragmented social work thinking. It is concerned with the nature of the situation to be dealt with rather than the social worker's skill and activity. By centering interest on common

---

[21] Elizabeth P. Rice, "Concepts of Prevention as Applied to the Practice of Social Work," *American Journal of Public Health,* Vol. 52, No. 2 (Feb-ruary 1962), pp. 266–274.

[22] Harriett M. Bartlett, *Social Work Practice in the Health Field* (New York: National Association of Social Workers, 1961), pp. 150–168.

(rather than unique) problems, it moves social work toward its area of central concern, away from the divisive thinking so frequently found in earlier days. It broadens the scope of thinking. For social work it is a new avenue to understanding human behavior and leads to developing new clusters of knowledge.[23]

The Concept of Coping

The idea of task leads directly to the idea of coping. They go together. Having identified and described the nature of life tasks, we must then try to answer the question of how people actually deal with these tasks. Again, the concept is a broad one, having to do with typical patterns of response and action applicable to many people.

Social work thinking in general and casework in particular have directed attention to problems and problem-solving, with special concern for people who have difficulty in solving their problems of living. Because of the dependence on psychiatric theory, there has been an emphasis on emotional, irrational, and unconscious aspects of behavior, which frequently result in evasion and denial and thus temporary or prolonged avoidance of life tasks. In contrast, the emerging concept of coping now emphasizes the conscious, cognitive, and rational aspects of behavior also. In such behavior there is usually a direct engagement with the situation and coping can then be described as relative mastery of the tasks involved in the situation.[24] It is recognized that most people will

---

[23] After the approach to the concept of social functioning presented in this chapter had been developed and formulated, the writer read a paper by Elliot Studt, "Social Work Theory and Implications for the Practice of Methods," *Social Work Education Reporter,* Vol. 16, No. 2 (June 1968), pp. 22–24 and 42–46, which discusses theory about social work practice derived from research done in a special correctional unit for young offenders. In her paper Studt presents concepts of *tasks* and *situation,* regarded as relevant for all social work practice, that have many points of similarity with those developed independently by the writer of this monograph.

[24] Lois Barclay Murphy and collaborators, *The Widening World of Childhood* (New York: Basic Books, 1962); and Lydia Rapoport, "Crisis-Oriented Short-Term Casework," *Social Service Review,* Vol. 41, No. 1 (March 1967), pp. 39–40.

suffer stress in dealing with the tasks but that some will be able to take the necessary steps without becoming excessively disturbed or disorganized. It is further recognized that other people fail in life tasks, not through any weakness in themselves, but through lack of opportunity to learn the appropriate behavior or essential social skills, that is, from not having had the kind of life experiences that would prepare them to take the necessary steps. The Head Start projects, which provide such missing experiences for deprived preschool children, aim to fill this gap through direct teaching and learning in order to increase the coping capacity of the children when they move into formal education.[25]

When the demands of the environment are excessive in relation to the coping capacities of the people involved in the situation, then coping becomes ineffectual and the people become helpless and overwhelmed. Poverty, racial discrimination, lack of access to jobs, and other societal problems subject large segments of the population to stress, anxiety, deprivation, and alienation. Here, of course, major efforts for social change must be directed at the environment. In spite of the recognized inadequacy of people's coping in such situations, social workers want to make sure that the people themselves have a part in the planning and action that affect their welfare so that they can maintain positive interaction with the social environment. As the pressures of the environment can be lessened, the coping efforts of the people can become more effective and successful.

Some social workers, recognizing the inadequacy of society's provisions for large groups in the population, might consider the concept of coping irrelevant because these people are helpless in dealing with their own situations. The concept is important, however, even in extreme situations, because it emphasizes a concern and respect for people's strivings toward attainment of their own potential, in line with social work's basic values. It underlines the importance of people's being active and sharing in planning for their own future. Lacking such a concept, social workers could again fall into the error that plagued the field in the early

---

[25] These projects, developed as part of the federal antipoverty programs during the Johnson Administration, offer special opportunities and training to preschool children from deprived homes with the aim of preparing them better for entrance into school.

days of casework, namely, that of *doing for* people, which leads to manipulation and domination.

The manner in which these concepts of task and coping are being incorporated in practice is demonstrated by the writing of Silverman. Describing services for the widowed during bereavement, she says: "The conceptual scheme by which most of us examine the problems of our clients leads us to seek the etiology of these problems in their early childhood experiences." The service that has been available—casework—is designed to help the client with his malfunctioning, which is viewed as a reflection of personality or interpersonal difficulties resulting from his psychosocial development. She then goes on to analyze the experience of bereavement as a "critical transition" with a beginning and end, between which the individual does "the work of the transition." Traditionally, casework has emphasized the client's defensive behavior and emotional state. To deal with these problems in terms of the individual's past adjustment, Silverman points out, will not be as effective as dealing with them as a stage in the transition that he will experience and with which—with time and mastery of the current situation—he will be able to cope.[26]

Silverman demonstrates progress from casework's earlier emphasis on the psychogenetic history of the individual to a concern with current coping efforts directed toward life tasks—what she calls "the work of the transition"—that are common to many or all people. The change of focus allows social work thinking to move beyond the single idea of individualizing the client to generalizing about people's coping efforts, as in relation to widowhood, and thus toward a broader view of behavior.

A Concept of Social Functioning for Social Work

Now it is possible to return to the question raised at the beginning of this chapter regarding the central focus of social work as a profession. The emerging concepts of task and coping are

---

[26] Phyllis Rolfe Silverman, "Services for the Widowed During the Period of Bereavement," *Social Work Practice, 1966* (New York: Columbia University Press, 1966), pp. 170 and 177.

useful in suggesting a comprehensive concept to identify the professional focus. Coping refers to people's actions in striving to meet and actually deal with situations that may be variously conceived as social tasks, life situations, or problems of living. People experience these life tasks primarily as pressures from their social environment.[27] Two major ideas come out of this: *people coping,* on the one hand, and *environmental demands,* on the other. To become parts of a single comprehensive concept, these ideas must be brought together within the same dimension and it is the idea of *social interaction* that the writer thinks accomplishes this.[28]

Social workers are concerned both with people's opportunity to grow and with obstacles to attainment of full potential. Thus in considering the interaction between people and environment, they must bear in mind the *consequences* of this interaction for people's growth. Are the environmental demands excessive?

----

[27] The idea of task has been useful in freeing social workers from old limitations of thinking but is not in itself broad enough to become a major term in a central social work concept. It continues to be needed, however, as a subconcept for clarifying the nature of environmental demands.

[28] William E. Gordon took the first step in linking "coping capacity" and "environmental demand" within a single concept through the idea of "match or mismatch" between capacity or demand, in a memo to the Experimental Field Instruction staff, George Warren Brown School of Social Work, Washington University, St. Louis, Missouri, December 4, 1963. Previously, other aspects of social functioning had been emphasized, as shown by J. O. Jacques Alary, in a meaning analysis of the expression "social functioning" as a social work concept, which he reported in 1968. In an analysis of 416 statements concerning social functioning, appearing in 162 articles published in *Social Work* and *Social Casework* between 1956 and 1967, he found that the dominant tendency was to conceptualize social functioning at a low level of abstraction and to use it to designate a behavioral phenomenon. The individual human person is the most frequent system to which "social functioning" is ascribed as a property. Environmental factors identified as having some influence on the social functioning of individuals are designated by terms that lack determinacy of meaning. The nature of the qualifiers used suggests that social functioning corresponds most often to a clinical entity whose manifestations are to be diagnosed and evaluated. Only a few qualifiers suggested other dimensions. *See* J. O. Jacques Alary, "A Meaning Analysis of the Expression 'Social Functioning' as a Social Work Concept," pp. 106–107. Unpublished doctoral dissertation, Tulane University, December 1967.

Are people's coping capacities inadequate? If there is imbalance, how can the *balance* be improved? Since we are concerned with growth and potential, which imply ongoing change, it is important that any balance attained, at any particular time, should not be rigid but flexible.[29] The consequences of early coping efforts may enable people to enlarge their efforts and so improve their coping that they succeed in meeting the environmental demands. On the other hand, if coping efforts are persistently inadequate, disorganization may ensue and the people may become overwhelmed by the situation.

Examination of the Concept

How does such a central concept for social work meet the requirements set forth earlier? This interpretation of social functioning has the possibility of providing what social work has never had—a concept broad enough to encompass the profession's scope and yet clear enough to provide a focus that will stimulate integrated thinking and effort. It is a positive way of limiting the profession's area of interest without having to set outer boundaries and is a way of defining what social work is that is sufficiently open ended to allow for further development.

The essential ideas in this comprehensive concept describing the profession's focus are, at the most abstract level, *the interaction of people and environment.* They can be expressed thus:

People ←——→ **Interaction** ←——→ **Environment**

So expressed, the concept is too impersonal for a service profession like social work, which is concerned with helping people to deal with their life situations in various ways. To accomplish their goal, social workers must understand the meaning of the situations to the people involved in them. Thus to be more

---

[29] *See* the use of the idea of *balance* by M. Antoinette Cannon as quoted on page 88, and also by Margaret L. Schutz, "Report of the Field Instruction Experimental Project of the George Warren Brown School of Social Work," pp. 3–4. Paper presented at the Annual Program Meeting, Council on Social Work Education, New York, New York, January 1966. (Mimeographed.)

suitable for social work, the concept may be elaborated and expressed thus:

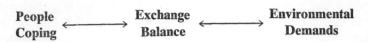

People
Coping ⟷ Exchange
Balance ⟷ Environmental
Demands

These ideas bring together several basic themes for the profession's focus. If the concept is to be genuinely integrative for the profession, it must be comprehensive. Until now most of the social work discussion of social functioning has centered around individuals and families.[30] In this monograph the suggested concept is extended to refer to "people" (whether as individuals or as groups) in order to cover social work practice more fully.[31]

To be comprehensive, the concept must also tie social work's central concerns more closely together. It was the failure to bring the ideas of people and environment together and hold them there that produced such a long lag in social work thinking. In the past there was a hiatus between the idea of the person and the idea of environment that blocked integrative thinking about the profession's focus. In individual situations, for instance, social workers talked of using ego psychology on the one side and knowledge of community resources on the other; but they are of different dimensions. We make progress in closing the gap when the interaction between people and environment is perceived as an active exchange. Often intensive effort will be required to identify the nature of the exchange between people and environment that is crucial in the particular situation. Having obtained

---

[30] Alary, op. cit.

[31] After this chapter was written, the writer found a paper by Marjorie M. McQueen, "The Role of the Social Worker in the Remediation of Children with 'Learning Disabilities,'" Patterns for Innovative Practice: School Social Work Conference (La Grange, Ill.: School Social Work Conference, 1967), pp. 59–68. In this paper McQueen presents a conceptual and diagrammatic analysis of social work practice based on people coping with environmental demands, which has many similarities to that presented here. Since she indicates that she is incorporating the thinking of Gordon and Bartlett, particularly from the writer's paper—"Characteristics of Social Work," Building Social Work Knowledge: Report of a Conference (New York: National Association of Social Workers, 1965)—it is not unexpected to find that our thinking should come together in this way.

such understanding, the social worker can then move to improve the balance between the people's coping efforts and the environmental demands. This may be done by working with people or environment but most frequently with both and always with concern for the interaction between them. It should be remembered that the ultimate goal of all this social work activity is the growth of the individual.

Several theoretical concepts are relevant and important for the refinement of this concept of social functioning. The idea of balance between the demands of the environment and the coping efforts of people is related to the concept of *homeostasis*, which was developed by Cannon and others to describe the maintenance of a steady state in the internal environment of the human body, through adjustment to various inner and outer threatening events.[32] This steady state is essential for the growth of the human organism, since sudden changes beyond the capacity of the system for self-regulation are disruptive, as has been shown in studies of stress.[33] Similarly in our concept of social functioning, if there is imbalance in the people-environment exchange, stress may result for people, environment, or both.

The interaction of people with their social environment may also be perceived as an open-ended social system. Thus social workers interested in systems theory can explore its contribution to the development of the social functioning concept. Since social workers are concerned with the consequences of interaction, the idea of *feedback* from systems theory is useful. In presenting systems theory for social workers, Hearn quotes Wiener's statement that "feedback is the property of being able to adjust future conduct by past performance." It may be used not only to regulate specific movements but also wider aspects of behavior.[34]

---

[32] Walter B. Cannon, *The Wisdom of the Body* (2d ed.; New York: W. W. Norton & Co., 1939).

[33] Hans Selye, *The Stress of Life* (New York: McGraw-Hill Book Co., 1956).

[34] Norbert Wiener, *The Human Use of Human Beings* (New York: Doubleday & Co., Anchor Books, 1954), p. 33, as quoted in Gordon Hearn, *Theory Building in Social Work* (Toronto, Canada: University of Toronto Press, 1958), p. 47. In relation to social systems theory for social work, *see also* Gordon Hearn, ed., *The General Systems Approach: Contributions Toward an Holistic Conception of Social Work* (New York: Council on Social Work Education, 1969).

Thus when people are coping with environmental demands, the feedback from this exchange may cause them to respond with increased effort, discovery of new resources, and such improvement of their coping that they succeed in meeting the demands and develop their own potential at the same time. On the other hand, if the feedback is negative, if people lack the means to respond, they may fail and be worse off than ever. The same may be true of the environment, which also responds to positive or negative feedback from the exchange. The essential point here is that encounters between people and environment leave both changed, and people and environments that lack restorative capacity may be adversely affected.[35]

Because the idea of social functioning is being widely used at present to refer to the central area of social work's concern, this term is being used here. It has been used with various meanings inside and outside social work. At one extreme it is used in a broad sense to describe wide areas of human behavior and extensive social phenomena with which many professions and disciplines are concerned. In social work it is frequently used to refer to the functioning of people in their social roles and relationships, with varying emphasis on their relation to the environment.[36] The gain made in the new concept suggested here is that it focuses not on the behavior of people, but on the exchanges between them and their environment, thus becoming a more dynamic concept with greater potential and power.

The Environmental Component

This concept of social functioning requires that social workers should be more concerned than they have been in the past with

---

[35] William E. Gordon, "Basic Constructs for an Integrative and Generative Conception of Social Work, in Hearn, ed., *op. cit.,* p. 8.

[36] It is the writer's opinion that the use of such a central concept to describe the profession's central focus would be a great advance in clarification and movement toward integrative thinking. If experience shows that the term "social functioning" cannot be used without continually reverting to earlier or narrower meanings, it may be better to use some new term. In the end, *the term is less important than the ideas.* Rather than arguing over "what is meant by social functioning," it will be more profitable to push toward new integrative concepts suitable for defining the social work focus.

the social environment as an entity to be understood and dealt with. Traditionally, knowledge about personality and group process has claimed greater attention than the environment. The manner in which the social environment operates to bring pressures upon people needs to be better understood. This is not the same thing as obtaining general knowledge about social conditions and social problems or knowledge that will enable social workers themselves to operate in the power structure. To be brought within the concept of social functioning, this knowledge must analyze and clarify the impact of the social environment on people, whether as individuals, groups, or communities. If coping efforts are to become effective, the nature of the pressures, stresses, and tasks must be better understood.

Furthermore, social workers must concern themselves with the people who comprise the environment because the consequences of social functioning affect them too. To some degree, social workers have extended their helping efforts to include others in the environment, as in extending help to the client's family. There has also been awareness that excessive concentration on the needs of clients could lead to the breakdown of others in the situation. What is now involved is a much more extensive phenomenon, namely, that changes brought about in the balance between the coping efforts of a group and the demands of their social environment can at times operate in such a way as to be seriously dysfunctional for some or all of the people in that environment. When low-income families were brought into housing projects, the purpose was to improve their living conditions. Only later was it recognized that when a considerable number of disorganized families were introduced into a project, their interaction with more stable families could initiate a process of deterioration extending throughout the project, thus creating a new and larger problem. The concept of social functioning calls for knowledge about and concern for the welfare of persons on both sides of the interaction.

In assessing the demands of the environment, it will also be necessary to identify the supports that it gives to the coping efforts of people. Social workers commonly think of these supports in terms of community resources and social welfare programs. The fact that social workers know these community resources and how to mobilize them is frequently mentioned as a major aspect of social work expertise. Until recently, less attention has been directed toward other more subtle but powerful community forces, such as the operation of political organizations and sociocultural attitudes. These are of basic importance in either the support or rejection they offer to various groups living in the community. The widespread attitude in American society that economic dependency is a sign of personal failure is, for instance, demeaning to the people who must seek public support. The increasing inability of urban governments to provide necessary social services to deprived groups in the inner city has become a major problem of our times. In such ways the social environment fails to meet the needs of large segments of the population and places demands upon them that are far beyond the limits of their coping capacity.

Implications for Knowledge-building

As we strive to identify a central concept for social work, we perceive how these efforts also contribute to building social work knowledge. These ideas have to do with tasks, problems, and demands that must be met by many people. What they require of people in the way of response can be described with considerable precision as to the nature of the impact and requirement. Also the coping behavior of people can be described and patterns of coping can be identified. After a suitable period of study, one would hope that coping patterns associated with certain tasks and environmental demands and the interchange involved can be identified, just as Lindemann was able to describe what he called "grief work" in relation to the experience of bereavement.[37]

This is a knowledge-building process. What social workers have not perceived clearly is that the various concepts, propositions, and generalizations useful and appropriate for their profession must be formulated as a body of knowledge so that they may be used most effectively in teaching and practice. As soon as it is recognized that knowledge-building must be a basic process,

---

[37] *Op. cit.*

the propositions and knowledge clusters with which social workers are familiar and that have been most actively used in the past can be brought together. To these can be added the new knowledge acquired by progressive study as described previously.

It is important not to underestimate the demands of such an undertaking, which will require hard, persistent work by many social workers over many years in clarifying concepts, defining entities, and developing and testing hypotheses. There is, however, a particular challenge and opportunity in that this search falls squarely in social work's domain and is less likely to be undertaken by other professions or disciplines.

As part of a long train of thought originating in the Working Definition, Gordon has given concentrated attention to the development of basic constructs that are similar to those now emerging in social work but more rigorously developed and formulated. "The ideas," he says, "should be integrative in the sense of capturing the common elements across the varied practice of social work today without the loss of historical continuity. They should be generative in the sense of moving the profession's thinking forward in step with the future." The following is a key paragraph from his formulation:

Following this form of construction we can say quite simply that the central concern of social work technology is the *matching of people's coping patterns with the qualities of impinging environment for the purpose of producing growth inducing and environment ameliorating transactions.* This in a crude way social work actually seems to have been trying to do with such knowledge as is available from related disciplines and its own experience, but without a rationalizing conceptualization such as the above. I say rationalizing conceptualization deliberately since it is all I have so far given. Social work practice has been and will continue to be dependent upon bits of theory from many sources, applied non-theoretically until such time as it has as a minimum some set of rationalizing constructs capable of spanning the breadth of its concern for man where he lives day in and day out and in terms of what the outcomes are for him and his environment for the remainder of his life. No other profession or discipline

108   THE COMMON BASE OF SOCIAL WORK PRACTICE

claiming any recourse to specialized science sets goals with such current breadth and temporal length, and no currently available behavioral science attempts to span that breadth and length. To claim at this point in history to be a scientific practice places social work in jeopardy of adopting a scientific approach far too narrow or limited to carry the breadth and length of its aspirations and its practice in the behalf of these aspirations for people. To maintain itself as even a modern technology, social work must at least have a frame of reference which rationalizes the connection between its goals for people and society and the base of its claimed expertise. To become a science it must obviously have more. To become a science in the particular frame of reference above would require studying and establishing the following:

(1) The relationship between combinations of coping patterns and environmental demands and the kind and amount of exchange taking place, and

(2) The relationship between these exchanges and the growth and development of the individual and the amelioration of the environment—in other words, a scientific understanding of the transaction intersystem.[38]

Gordon has for some time suggested that social work can and should develop its own science and that its knowledge should rest on such a scientific base. Some social workers think that social work theory is not possible or desirable for social workers to attempt. Many prefer to look outside social work for theory. Others (including the writer) think that it has not been possible in the past because social workers' thinking has been so fragmented or diffused but may become possible as a more disciplined integrative approach is sought.

Social workers are accustomed to speak of their "practice knowledge," which is derived from and immediately useful in practice. Dubos comments on the use of knowledge in practice as follows:

---

[38] William E. Gordon, "Basic Constructs for an Integrative and Generative Conception of Social Work," pp. 7–8. Paper prepared for Workshop 60, Council on Social Work Education Annual Meeting, Minneapolis, Minnesota, January 26, 1968. (Mimeographed.)

The kind of knowledge most likely to have permanent value and to be useful in practice is theoretical knowledge. Even though it appears of no practical use at the time it is acquired, theoretical knowledge is the most useful for the future because it is applicable to a wide range of conditions. In any given field, the leaders are rarely those who have entered professional life with the largest amount of practical information, but rather those who have breadth of understanding, critical judgment, and especially discipline of learning. The intellectual equipment most needed is that which makes it possible to adapt rapidly to new situations, as they constantly arise in the ever-changing world.[39]

Social workers have perhaps not given enough thought to the point that theoretical knowledge may actually be the most useful kind to possess in a rapidly changing society.

In the past many social workers have resisted attempts to break apart the "whole person" or the "whole situation." But whole individuals, groups, or situations are extremely complex entities and not readily used as units of knowledge. All professions and disciplines have had to analyze and partialize the social situation and the behavior of the individual in some way for purposes of understanding. Thus better understanding of social functioning, viewed as coping behavior in relation to life tasks and environmental demands, does not conflict with the characteristic social work approach. Social workers will still be working with people as individuals or groups but will be giving more effective help because of their better understanding of needs and problems.

A Systematic Approach to Knowledge

New directions for movement toward systematic knowledge-building will open up when social work has actually identified its own focus. Then there will be understanding of what educators call "the structure of a subject," the central theme and the manner in which other concerns are related to it.[40] Once such a central

---

[39] René Dubos, *Man Adapting* (New Haven: Yale University Press, 1967), p. 425.

[40] Jerome S. Bruner, *The Process of Education* (New York: Vintage Books, 1963), pp. 6–11.

focus is recognized and used, the knowledge most essential for and distinctive to social work can be accumulated. The contributions from various individual researchers will each reinforce the other instead of remaining unconnected. Social work thinking will then become more cumulative.

Social workers have been in too great a hurry to put their fragmented and incomplete knowledge to work immediately in the form of skill, method, and action. In the effort to help people deal with their problems and make the environment more responsive to people's needs, for a prolonged period there was concentration on individualizing the particular situation, with the use of such knowledge as could be readily assembled from existing sources. The development of the idea that the goal of social work is the "enhancement of social functioning" broadened the approach but still kept the concept of social functioning tied primarily to social work action. If social functioning is to be enhanced, then criteria for *effective* functioning become necessary. Under these circumstances, the concept covers not only what *is* but what *ought to be,* namely, norms and values as well as knowledge, and this has proved difficult to handle. Thus social workers have become involved in the risk of imposing, often unconsciously and unintentionally, their own social work values, middle-class values, or requirements for conformity to societal expectations.

Going back to the earlier discussion of knowledge and value, it is suggested that in the development and use of an integrative concept for social work, the principles developed there should be followed: (1) knowledge and value should be given priority over interventive action and (2) the distinction between knowledge and value should be maintained.[41] Many practitioners may feel that in working with people in particular situations, their goals

---

[41] In tracing the development of the expression "social functioning," Alary found that in the early social work literature the dominant concept was "social adjustment." Around 1940, a change was made to the expression "social functioning." Special problems of conceptualization were presented to social workers in relation to the normative implications of social adjustment and these were carried over to the concept of social functioning by many writers, who assumed a built-in reference to conformity with social norms. A minority of writers regarded social functioning as implicitly neutral social transactions judged by consequences for human realization and effect on environment. Alary, *op. cit.,* pp. 32, 59, and 131.

actually can be described as bringing about more effective social functioning. For professional practice as a whole, however, at this stage in its development, a more discriminating formulation, which clarifies how the essential elements are to be used in relation to each other, is needed.

What is being suggested is that primary emphasis should be given to developing and testing knowledge propositions that are relevant for social work practice and useful for all practitioners. This means that the overall concept of social functioning, as developed here, is to be regarded as neutral and not incorporating normative criteria. Gordon describes this approach as follows:

> Social functioning, for some time considered the ultimate concern of social work, becomes the beginning, not the end of social work interest, an interest fed by the impact of functioning patterns on both human growth and the social environment. Knowledge pursued and formulated along the feedback lines of social functioning to the individual and to his environment is a neglected area of inquiry largely untouched by psychologies and sociologies that are intent on explaining the causes of social functioning rather than its consequences.[42]

Thus patterns of coping, patterns of environmental demand, and the relationships between them should be studied as rigorously and objectively as possible. The consequences of the exchanges are also to be studied, using the ideas of balance, feedback, and other relevant concepts to determine their impact on people and their environment.

In this approach, the purpose of studying social functioning is not to define certain types of functioning as good or desirable, but simply to *understand* the various components, their relationships, and the outcomes. As more adequate knowledge regarding social functioning is built up by the profession, practitioners will be better able to foresee the possible and probable consequences of the various patterns of exchange between people and environment. In working with neighborhood groups, for instance, they will learn what kinds of participation in various projects, under what cir-

---

[42] Gordon, "Knowledge and Value: Their Distinction and Relationship in Clarifying Social Work Practice," p. 39.

cumstances, are likely to lead to positive or destructive results for all involved.

As knowledge becomes a more adequate instrument for understanding, values in their turn can be put to better use. In our changing society, we are as yet hardly prepared to deal with questions of what patterns of social functioning will be most likely to contribute to human growth and potential. Decisions as to what is effective functioning for people, viewed in terms of human growth, can only be made by a helping profession in association with the people themselves. The kinds of balanced exchanges between people and environment that contribute most to human potential will be gradually learned when social workers work with people as participant-observers, share their thinking, and continually study the various patterns of coping, demand, and exchange in relation to their human consequences.

This means that knowledge and values are constantly used together but kept separate. Broad integrative *knowledge* concepts, such as social functioning, are associated with growing bodies of knowledge. Broad integrative *value* concepts, such as the realization of human potential, are associated with growing bodies of values. It is through the professional judgment of practitioners that knowledge and value are applied in specific situations, an aspect of practice to be discussed later. Meanwhile—and this is the important point of the discussion—concepts and propositions that merge what *is* with what *ought to be* should be avoided. They are confusing because values by their very nature must be left open to varying interpretations. Furthermore, if value and knowledge become locked in rigid concepts, the profession may not be free to recognize and use new knowledge as it develops.

Would it be clearer to describe the concern and responsibility of social work not as enhancement of social functioning or effective social functioning, but as *understanding* of social functioning to permit the fullest and freest use of knowledge and values regarding outcomes of exchanges between people and environment in terms of their import for human potential and the social environment? Better formulations will undoubtedly be developed. The need is for better ways of articulating the problems that would clarify how social work knowledge and value are used together without a kind of premature merging that leads to bias and confusion in professional judgments, concepts, and goals.

Value of an Integrated Approach

This approach to knowledge-building emphasizes social work's central and distinctive knowledge and regards the building of this central knowledge as crucial for the profession's effective contribution. Use of integrative concepts which clarify the profession's focus will offer a solution for the difficulty that has plagued social work throughout its history and continues to baffle it. It has always been clear that social work must and should draw knowledge and theory relevant to its practice from related professions and disciplines. At first this was done irregularly, as has been described, with a bias in one direction or another and without full integration of the selected material. Recently it has been recognized that this process must be accomplished in a more orderly and disciplined manner. But meanwhile, the sources from which such knowledge must come have been expanding to an almost unmanageable degree. The list began with psychiatry and psychology from the behavioral sciences and sociology, economics, anthropology, and social psychology from the social sciences. Now political science and public administration have been added. In addition, clusters of theory relating to specific aspects of behavior and social structure, such as small-group and organizational theory, are relevant. Among the professions, social work has always drawn from the health, legal, and teaching professions as well as the ministry. With current social change, still other occupational groups whose interests overlap with those of social work, such as urban planners, are emerging. The new approach will provide for a clearer selection of relevant knowledge from these other sources and, what is particularly important, a better relating of this knowledge to social work's concerns.

More progress can also be made in clarifying social work's "practice wisdom," which continues to lie imbedded in its practice with only limited formulation and testing. Because of their close working relationships with people in difficulty, social workers are acquiring a kind of understanding not available to or sought by other professions and disciplines of what the problems mean to people and the nature of their coping efforts. Such potential knowledge—for example, that relating to a public welfare system which incorporates an attitude of blaming recipients for their predicament and thus regards them as unworthy of respect—is timely, even urgently needed, in today's society. Better recognition of the profession's focus and the process of knowledge-building will permit the designing of projects through which the knowledge imbedded in practice can be obtained and tested.

Thus definition of a comprehensive concept of social functioning will stimulate and promote the development of social work's characteristic knowledge derived from its past and future experience. It will also facilitate and guide the selection and use of generalizations from other professions and disciplines that are relevant for social work. Both types of knowledge can then be incorporated into the profession's common body of knowledge in a planned and orderly manner not possible before.

Unintegrated Segments of Knowledge

A clarified focus will not only contribute to building the central body of knowledge but also make possible the bringing together of segments of new knowledge previously isolated from each other in various areas of the profession's practice. In the discussion of the fields in the opening chapter, it was pointed out how social workers in the early days of the profession perceived the central problem of their concern to be the one specific to their area of practice, such as health or child welfare. As the movement to develop a description of the social work focus gains momentum, practitioners will perceive themselves as social workers first and only second as workers in one or another field of practice. This change in perception moves the overall concept of social functioning to the forefront and gives it priority. When this occurs, social workers will perceive the situations with which they deal first as manifestations of social functioning and only secondarily as falling into particular types of social functioning, such as family problems or correctional problems. Knowledge needed in the various fields of practice can be brought together under one frame of reference, that is, social work. What is relevant for all social workers then can flow into social work's general body of knowledge and what is specific to the field can remain as specialized knowledge.

Another segment of social work knowledge is the kind that has become submerged in the three methods. All social workers need knowledge about individuals, groups, and the community that is related to their social functioning but not limited to particular interventive measures. In the same way that knowledge related to the fields of practice became tied to a specific field, the knowledge submerged in each practice method became imbedded in the method. But what can and should be known and used by all social workers can be lifted out and reorganized to make it visible and available within the profession's overall body of knowledge. Further refinement of criteria for selection and experimentation in their application will, of course, be required. As the focus is clarified, there will be the advantage that instead of being hidden within fields and methods, new knowledge can find its appropriate place in the growing body of knowledge belonging to the whole profession.

A third segment of unintegrated social work knowledge has to do with a wide range of activities that are related but supplementary to professional social work practice. Undoubtedly, social workers need to know a great deal about foster homes, child care centers, homemakers, nursing homes, and other such services; quite possibly more knowledge is available in the literature about these phases of practice than about the central area of social functioning. Some people propose to build social work knowledge by collecting and coding all that is now formulated. A basic point of this discussion is, however, that the effective organization and use of such supplementary knowledge depends upon the clarification of the profession's central focus. Priority should be given to establishing and encouraging a continuous effort to build social work knowledge *at its center,* since all the rest depends on achieving progress there.

The Social Functioning Concept: A Recapitulation

Because the suggested concept of social functioning represents a somewhat unfamiliar approach, it seems well to restate the main outlines of the proposition at this point. The concept rests on the general idea of interaction between people and environment. To make it suitable for social work, it is further refined and focused on the relation between the coping activity of people and the demands of environment. Many earlier interpretations of social functioning centered on the functioning of individuals or groups, that is, on behavior. This concept differs in that attention is now directed primarily to what goes on *between* people and environment through the exchange between them. This dual focus ties them together. Thus person and situation, people and environment, are encompassed in a single concept, which requires that they be constantly viewed together.

The interaction between coping efforts and environmental demands can be regarded as a field of multiple interweaving actions. What the social worker wants to understand particularly for dealing with the situation is the balance (or, as Gordon says, the "matching") between coping and demands. Here we are concerned not with crude activities but with their interrelationships in order to understand further their consequences for the growth of people and the amelioration of their environment. We do not yet have concepts to describe the nature of this exchange and balance, that is, what passes between people and their environment. What is going on is not "exchanging behavior" but something more vital and significant for people's growth. It is of a different order than behavior or activity and requires understanding of the changes that result from them.

Some of the questions and concerns regarding such an exchange might be the following: Is effective communication going on between people and their environment or is it being blocked? Is the transmission of feelings—whether aggressive or hostile, supportive or stimulating—the most significant aspect and what are the consequences of such a transmission? Does the exchange lead to the disorganization of people, the environment, or both? Does it involve a kind of participation that is growth producing for the people and perhaps equally positive and stimulating on both sides of the exchange? We need more refined concepts that will enable us to get at what is significant for human growth in these exchanges and in the balance or imbalance that results.

As was pointed out previously, the first step must be to understand the coping patterns, environmental demands, various kinds of exchange and balance, and their consequences, through rigorous study of situations and use of the growing body of knowledge. In this development and use of the social functioning concept, knowledge and values are to be kept separate and the concept's primary base is in knowledge.

As this knowledge grows, social work's goal of maximum realization for every individual will rest more firmly on knowledge and be better related to practice. Since the means for furthering this goal now involve many ways of working through other channels than working directly with the individual—as with neighborhood groups, social programs, and social policy—it is important to keep always in mind that it is the growth of individuals with which all this larger effort is ultimately concerned. That is, social workers in their intervention hope to influence the balance in the relationship between coping activity and environmental demands in order to further individual growth as well as ameliorate the environment.

The concept of social functioning, which has been growing and changing over several decades in social work practice, has not yet developed its full potential for defining the profession's focus. If it can be thought of as more than the behavior of individuals and can be extended to include their active and exchanging relationship with their environment along with the feedback and consequences to both flowing from that active relationship, more of its promise may be realized.[43]

In conclusion, in the preceding discussion a number of emerging ideas were identified and brought together in a concept of social functioning that has potential for clarifying the central focus of the profession. Hamilton pointed out that the strength of social work lies in its ability "to operate at both ends of the psychosocial event," in its refusal to limit itself to either external factors or internal factors alone.[44] The suggested concept of social functioning unites the "psychic" and the "social," as social work views them. If developed further, it could provide a much-needed anchor point for the profession.

---

[43] *See* Gordon, "Basic Constructs for an Integrative and Generative Conception of Social Work."

[44] Hamilton, "The Role of Social Casework in Social Policy," p. 33.

7

social work
orientation

Out of the discussion of social functioning, another characteristic permeating the practice comes to the surface and should be made explicit. In examining specific instances of practice, we observe that social workers characteristically begin by trying to understand a situation from the viewpoint of the people involved in it. They are searching for answers to such questions as the following: What is the impact of the situation on these people? What is its meaning for them? How are they coping with it? This is not, of course, the only orientation from which social work views the situation or intervenes. As a professional person, the social worker must seek an objective understanding of all relevant factors in the situation, which will encompass a broader view than that of the people involved. He is also concerned with the welfare of others in the immediate environment, such as family members and others interacting with those being helped. From a preventive viewpoint, he must give consideration to the problems of all persons suffering from the same difficulties as those with whom he is currently working. Further, he must be concerned with the planning groups involved in any situation and with the interests of the whole community.

Although this effort to understand the situation from the position and viewpoint of the people involved is thus not the only orientation, it can be described as primary and basic in that social workers seek it early and hold to it consistently. It applies in collaborative relationships as well as in direct services to individuals and groups, as will be shown later. Terms commonly used to describe this characteristic of any profession or group are "focus," "position," "perception," "view," "orientation," "perspective," and "stance." Having taken "focus" to mean the social work profession's area of central concern, we will now use "orientation" to mean the social worker's position and perspective in relation to the people and social phenomena in his practice. Two ideas are important in the concept of orientation. First we ask: Where does the observer stand? What is his position in relation to the social phenomena with which he is concerned? Second we ask: What is the particular angle or perspective from which he views the phenomena?

A helpful illustration comes from an interdisciplinary project that explored the possibility of a unified theory of human behavior. The project members had attempted (1) to identify the main elements in a particular discipline or field, (2) to construct some sort of model in which the main elements could be related to each other, and (3) to grapple with the problem of how interactions can take place, particularly how to get from one level to another. At this point, Jurgen Ruesch, one of the participants, suggested that there is a fourth essential factor—that the location of the observer also takes its place in the model. Observations in all sciences are made by an individual who has a position relative to his object, he pointed out. "He can only have one frame of reference at a time, although several can be put together through a mental operation. Natural events are viewed not in terms of the reality of the matter but through the eyes of an observer who is part of a specific communication system." [1] Confusion and misunderstanding result from failure to make clear the observer's position.

Thus for effective communication the position of the observer must be clear to all concerned. Where is he standing in relation to the phenomenon he is describing and with which he is dealing? Is he looking at it from the outside? If so, from what distance? Is he looking at it from the inside? If so, is he participating in the process himself and in what way? Members of academic disciplines usually aim to understand the phenomenon as objectively

---

[1] Roy R. Grinker, "Summary," in Grinker, ed., *Toward a Unified Theory of Human Behavior* (New York: Basic Books, 1956), pp. 126, 127, and 367.

and impersonally as possible, without influencing it or causing it to change. Members of helping professions, on the other hand, are necessarily part of the situations and processes they seek to change.

Where does the social worker stand? His primary and consistent view of the situation is, as has been suggested, in terms of its implications for the people involved in the problem.[2] We repeat that this is not his only orientation; but it is clearly a major one and a characteristic that is important for understanding the profession. Members of other professions and disciplines working with social workers observe this social work orientation and comment on it.[3] It was visible enough to be recognized by a reporter on a local newspaper who wrote about a counseling center in a military establishment, a setting not ordinarily regarded as compatible with the principles and goals of social work. The reporter wrote as follows:

> In an obscure corner of this military installation is a branch of the Army known as the Community Affairs Center. It is a new concept for the Army: one which was set up to counsel servicemen in any type of social problems.
>
> When you visit the center and enter the office of the man in charge you're faced with a desk piled high with important looking papers. A plaque on the desk reads, "Capt. Smith." Somehow you expect to see an older man, perhaps graying at the temples. But the eyes that look up from the mass of paperwork are young and alert. You are greeted by an impish grin and a boyish face. Donald Smith is in his mid-20s. He has a bright clean look about him. In a sport shirt and jeans you would expect to see him wolfing down hamburgers at a local drive-in. But in an officer's uniform, he looks a little out of place and you wonder if the university diploma

    [2] John C. Kidneigh, "History of American Social Work," *Encyclopedia of Social Work* (New York: National Association of Social Workers, 1965), p. 11.

    [3] Stanley H. King, *Perceptions of Illness and Medical Practice* (New York: Russell Sage Foundation, 1962), pp. 291–292; Irwin T. Sanders, "Professional Roles in Planned Change," in Robert Morris, ed., *Centrally Planned Change: Prospects and Concepts* (New York: National Association of Social Workers, 1964), pp. 104–110.

and the certificate from the National Association of Social Workers on the wall really belong to this fellow.

However, Donald Smith, despite his age and appearance, is a captain in the U.S. Army and a man sometimes responsible for holding families together. When he speaks of his job and describes the problems he must deal with, and when you see the concern he harbors, you know the documents on the wall bear the right name.

For Smith, the Community Service office is a step in the direction of social awareness by the Army. But Smith takes exception to the slogan, "The Army takes care of its own." "I think the office is the Army's recognition that maybe in today's society the Army can't take care of its own," Smith explains. However, he is quick to note, "It's not that the Army doesn't want to take care of its own, it's just that we can't run such things as an adoption agency, child care centers, or agencies for retarded children." According to Smith, the Army recognizes itself as a community with community problems.

The social worker went on to tell about several individual problems, including that of a pregnant wife who had overwhelming debts and an inductee who was found to have six children. The reporter's simple human interest story shows that he senses this young social worker's basic concern for the people he serves and realizes why the army, in spite of its great authority and enormous resources, cannot itself meet their needs but must have the assistance of a relatively little-known and little-understood profession.

Social Work Orientation to People

In early social work, two orientations to the people they were helping were manifested by social workers. Social reformers worked to bring about improved social conditions on behalf of people who were not able to produce the necessary changes through their own unaided efforts. The other orientation, developed in social casework, was a helping relationship viewed as a disciplined, professional interpersonal process. Both approaches emphasized the worth and dignity of the human being and understanding his needs as a basis for action.

Largely around the client-worker relationship there grew up an important group of concepts and attitudes, previously discussed, that emphasized the client's self-determination, sensitivity to his feelings, shared goals, and effort to help him solve his problem in his own way without dominating him. This meant that social workers must learn to view the problem through the individual's eyes. It also meant that, as part of the professional relationship, they learned to accept the individual as a person without necessarily approving his behavior. This was a complex but extremely significant aspect of professional behavior that, once incorporated in the practitioner, became of major importance for all future practice. It is an important characteristic for a profession because so much of the intolerance in today's society results from the condemnation of other people's actions as unacceptable without the ability to understand and accept them simply as human beings.

In the agencies in which they were employed, social workers worked with many other kinds of personnel, such as members of the administrative staff and members of other professions involved in giving service to clients. They also worked with the staff of agencies in the community to obtain services for their clients. This required an understanding of the nature of their working relationships with these other personnel and a management of these relationships that would contribute to better service to clients.

In traditional social work practice, the attainment of consensus, good teamwork, and smooth working relationships were emphasized. Power and conflict were not directly or consciously used. However, in situations involving so many people, there are necessarily competing interests, crosscurrents, and different ways of defining what ought to be done. What social workers learned about handling their various orientations is important and needs to be recognized. Such situations arise particularly in institutions when another profession is predominant. When the client or patient is working smoothly with the professional staff and the agency program, the problem does not arise. Not infrequently, however, serious rifts open up. Sometimes the client resists agency policy and procedure or cannot accept the leadership and authority of the teacher, physician, or other professional person. Years ago, Plant pointed out that there are always individuals who have difficulty in working successfully with social institutions and who need someone who is part of the setting but separate enough so that they can talk freely of their troubles in working with the institution. This is an important role of social work when it is part of a larger institution.[4]

In these situations there is a general pattern of changing relationships that social workers aim to follow, although many, of course, succeed only partially. When individuals have difficulty with the institution, the social worker moves temporarily toward the client or patient and away from the professional staff in order to give the person freedom to express his difficulties. The social worker is able to accept the expression of hostility, recognizing that it is not directed at him personally. The social worker, however, does not go so far as to relinquish his identification with the other professionals and the agency; nor does he permit the individual to go so far that he puts himself beyond the bounds of help. The social worker's goal is to enable the individual and the institution to come together again in a more effective working relationship. Since he cannot be in more than one position at a time, in such conflict situations the social worker moves back and forth between the individual who is receiving the service and those on the agency staff who are giving the service, listening to the individual's difficulties and then interpreting them to the staff. While there must be a temporary shift in identification with either the individual or staff, and the change in position can be quite marked at times, the social worker never relinquishes his basic identification with the individual or his place on the staff that is giving the service.

The same kind of movement takes place when social workers in one program are trying to obtain service from other agencies and programs. This may be an individual referral or an effort to expand services for a whole group. On the one hand, the social worker may work with individuals or groups to increase their social skills in seeking and using the service, as when adolescents are prepared to apply for jobs through an employment agency. On the

---

[4] James S. Plant, *Personality and the Cultural Pattern* (New York: Commonwealth Fund, 1937).

other hand, the social worker takes action to interpret the needs of the people involved in the problem to the other agency. In this process the social worker maintains his interest in and identification with both client and agency, making this clear to both. If the social worker were to exert continuing heavy pressure on the other agency and to show a one-sided alignment with the client, he would be likely to fail in his efforts to influence the agency.

So much attention has been given in the social work literature to the direct working relationship with those being served and to what is called the "enabling process" in community organization that there has been insufficient analysis of this particular capacity of social workers for managing simultaneously a variety of orientations, often conflicting, with clients and others. Several points should be noted. The social worker is aware of the various orientations required and manages them consciously. He is flexible in moving from one to the other but maintains primary identification with the people being served, whether or not he is in direct contact with them. The orientation to all persons in the situation manifests that quality of acceptance and understanding without necessarily agreement or approval, which was described as developing first in casework. This is, then, an orientation that does not solve all problems but has been and can be effective in a large proportion of the situations occurring in the practice of a helping profession like social work. Hopefully, the rationale and dynamics of this way of functioning will be better understood as the profession grows and faces new issues of orientation.

Social Work Orientation to Knowledge

The primary social work orientation to people and their needs has been recognized and consciously applied in working with them and in collaborating with others. The implications for the helping process and social work as a helping profession have been understood and incorporated in practice. What has not been so clear is the implication for the profession's knowledge. The effort to understand what situations mean to people involved in them leads to a consistent pattern of thinking. This can be seen in the way the concept of social functioning is developing to encompass people's coping with environmental demands and the consequences for them. There is a concern for consequences, particularly in terms of human growth and potential. Thus social work needs to understand stress, response, the nature of effective and ineffective coping, the seeking and using of help, and similar phenomena. Social workers are acquiring such understanding from their experience in working with people in a wide range of life situations but, as has been indicated, little has as yet been translated into formal knowledge. Also, this understanding has been so mingled with value and method concepts that the true nature of the knowledge could not be distinguished.

The knowledge of a profession or discipline is amassed from some relatively consistent base and position in viewing the phenomena. The patterns of thinking are important because they are a major influence in knowledge-building. The analysis of the profession's focus in the preceding chapter led to the conclusion that the primary concern of social workers is with the social functioning of people, which they view as efforts to cope with life tasks and environmental demands. The social worker consistently seeks to understand the situation from the viewpoint of the people involved in it, both their attitudes about it and its impact on them. What now becomes clear is that this focus applies not only to working with people but also to understanding them and their needs, to building up knowledge about them. Thus it appears that social work is developing its own *cognitive stance,* its distinctive *orientation toward knowledge.* This is "the position of the observer," in Ruesch's terms. It means that social work knowledge will focus not only on social functioning but also on the viewpoint and position of the people involved in the situation. It is within this perspective that observations are made, concepts defined, and generalizations formulated. Such a focus and orientation are not at present being sought by any other profession or discipline; thus if social work continues to build its knowledge in this way, it will command an increasingly distinctive body of professional knowledge.

New Issues

In the past when social workers perceived a social need, they concentrated on the needed service, viewed as a process, and the working relationship with the client or others directly involved in the situation. The orientation became part of each method. Thus the basic orientation to the people being helped was not recognized or formulated for social work practice as a whole. If social work's movement toward such a stance is confirmed, then the implications call for further consideration.

This means that all social workers—whether working with individuals, large or small groups, institutions, or programs—need to think of their primary orientation to the people involved in the problem before becoming committed to one or another line of action in specific situations. As attention is directed increasingly toward work with social programs and the social structure of society, many social workers will find themselves moving away from the people involved in the problems. The basic social work orientation can be visualized most clearly when the practitioner has direct contact with the people he is helping. In the past, when the social work stance took the form of a professional relationship with a single individual, it was easily seen and understood. Empathy with such a client develops through direct interpersonal communication, verbal and nonverbal. The social worker feels the stress of the situation himself through being a part of it. There is closeness to the client in many ways, through identification, communication, and an actual physical position.

However, the concept of basic orientation becomes difficult to follow in those phases of social planning and community organization that occur at a high level in the community, state, or nation, when the social worker may have no direct contact with the people involved in the problem. Here the social worker achieves his understanding through reports and through others in touch with the situation. His major working relationships are with members of community planning groups and agencies, including persons active in the political arena and power structure. Under these conditions, when the social worker does not have direct contact and relationship, the stance has to be understood in a different way. The social worker can and should still be close to the people involved in the problem through his empathy and understanding. His use of social work values and knowledge enables him to comprehend what the situation means to them and he maintains his concern for their social functioning even though he remains at a distance. His location is not physically near to them but it is still a "position" that enables him to keep close to them in another sense. In a major article on "the action intellectuals" who are contributing to the shaping of governmental policy, White describes Wilbur J. Cohen as having had a hand in virtually every piece of social legislation considered by the Congress. After all his years in the government, it is pointed out, Cohen had lost none of his humanitarian glow—"as though," an acquaintance once said, "he feels every person in the country who is home alone sick is his personal responsibility." There hardly could be a better illustration of the social work stance and the impact it can have when it is clearly demonstrated.[5]

Conclusion

What is here called the primary orientation to the people in the situation does not seem to be a separate element but a permeating characteristic of social work and its practice. It appears in two forms: (1) as an attitude toward and relationship with people and (2) as an approach to knowledge that emphasizes understanding situations in terms of their impact on and meaning for the people involved. Here the concept of social functioning, as defined in social work terms, becomes of particular importance. It follows that practitioners should develop awareness of the kinds of orientation characteristic of their profession, toward people and knowledge. This means not only the ability to manage these particular orientations but also to handle all the others in their practice in such a way that the primary orientation is kept consistently in the center. Changes and adjustments in practice need to be tested within this approach. A particularly difficult and important practice situation is one in which the social worker is working predominantly with institutions and the social structure without direct contact with the people who have the problems.

This combination of a central focus on social functioning with a primary orientation to the people in the situation is peculiar to social work, influenced particularly by the profession's values. Other orientations to social functioning would be possible. As used in social work, focus and orientation have become interdependent. They are as yet only partially defined, but their full definition should be pursued because they bid fair to identify two of the most distinctive characteristics of the profession.

---

[5] Theodore H. White, "In the Halls of Power," *Life*, June 9, 1967, p. 50.

8

moving toward
the common base

The "Working Definition of Social Work Practice" developed and exemplified the idea of progressive clarification and definition of social work practice. At the time it was published, the Working Definition itself was the most comprehensive and sustained effort yet undertaken in that direction. It appears to have stimulated further thinking but not to the degree that was hoped and its influence throughout the profession cannot be accurately assessed. Gordon's analysis of the original formulation and his further development of essential concepts have been major ongoing steps. They are basic for the thinking in this monograph and have been used by others in the social work literature.

Since it was concerned with social work as a profession, the Working Definition described the elements common to the practice as a whole. Starting from this foundation, this author has examined social workers' earlier thinking about their practice and considered how these ideas do or do not contribute to the progressive clarification of the common base of social work. An effort has been made to develop further those ideas that were potentially useful but had been only partially developed and to bring them into relationship with each other and to build in new ideas, essential to the general concept of a common base, when important gaps were found.

128

At the present stage of analysis, the diagram on page 130 suggests how the common base of social work might appear when a number of its major elements are brought together. This diagram resembles the one on essential elements presented in Chapter 5 (page 82) but includes additional aspects subsequently discussed.

We begin at the top of the diagram with the central focus on social functioning and the orientation to the people involved in the situation, since these are characteristics that identify social work. Next come the bodies of values and knowledge. The values are concerned with human potential and growth. The knowledge centers around social functioning, viewed from the social work orientation. The values and knowledge are in themselves a source of the profession's strength, since the values are translated into professional attitudes and the knowledge becomes a way of understanding people and situations. The values and knowledge guide the interventive action of social work practitioners. Since effective intervention depends on all the other elements, it is placed last in the diagram. This is different from traditional thinking about social work practice, which customarily began with the methods. The interventive repertoire is presented as a single concept, not divided into separate techniques, because it belongs to the whole profession. This diagram helps us to attain what was found to be essential for the meaningful analysis of practice—a *comprehensive* view.

It should be clear that in this approach the practice itself is not described as "generic." The common base of social work practice consists of concepts, generalizations, and principles relating to knowledge, value, and intervention, i.e., abstract ideas. Practitioners learn these "common elements" in school and apply them in their professional practice. The base is not the doing but what *underlies* the doing.

In the opening pages of this monograph (pages 16–18) certain steps were identified that need to be undertaken by the social work profession if it is to succeed in identifying its strengths and putting them to use in society. The first four of these were as follows: to view the entirety of social work practice, to identify the profession's focus, to bring the common elements together, and to recognize the limitations in social work thinking.

Starting with the first step—to view the entirety of social work practice—we need to ask why it is apparently so difficult for

FIGURE 2. THE COMMON BASE OF SOCIAL WORK PRACTICE

Central Focus

on

Social Functioning

People coping with life situations
Balance between demands of the social environment
and people's coping efforts

↓

Orientation

Primary concern for
people involved in the situation

↓

Body   Body
of   of
Values   *Knowledge*

Attitudes   Ways of
toward people_____ understanding

↓

Interventive Repertoire

Working with
individuals, groups, social organizations
directly and through collaborative action

social workers to take the necessary steps toward a perception of their practice as no longer fragmented. They were accustomed for decades to think of their practice in terms of agencies, fields, and methods. To break through these traditional barriers to a broader view and, particularly, to get out of what has been called the "methods box" is proving a slow and arduous undertaking.

Social work writers and committees sometimes begin their thinking with general comments on the profession and then retreat to some particular segment of practice, saying: "We will do the analysis in terms of the area of practice that we know best." [1] The assumption that there is a common base may be quickly passed over, without discussion or examination of its nature. There may be further assumptions that the characteristics of the particular segment of practice being discussed actually are representative of social work, an assumption that cannot be tested unless some fairly solid picture of the essential elements in practice has been offered.

The idea of a common base, as well as the term itself, is appearing with increasing frequency in the literature in relation to various aspects or segments of social work and its practice but not in relation to practice as a whole. Examples of such usages are "the knowledge base of social work," [2] "the common base of the profession," [3] "a knowledge base for professional practice," [4] and "to provide social work students with a common base." [5] The increasing use of such ideas, although more often applied to

---

[1] See, for example, Maurice J. Karpf, The Scientific Basis of Social Work: A Study in Family Case Work (New York: Columbia University Press, 1931); and Charlotte Towle, The Learner in Education for the Professions: As Seen in Education for Social Work (Chicago: University of Chicago Press, 1954). Towle says: "I attempt to present the raw material of the social casework educator's observations and tentative thinking on the individual learner in an educational process oriented, in so far as possible, to his needs and capacities, while holding to the profession's needs and responsibilities" (p. xix).

[2] Alfred Kadushin, "The Knowledge Base of Social Work," in Alfred J. Kahn, ed., Issues in American Social Work (New York: Columbia University Press, 1959), p. 39.

[3] Catherine Papell and Beulah Rothman, "Group Work's Contribution to a Common Method," Social Work Practice, 1966 (New York: Columbia University Press, 1966), p. 35.

[4] Mark P. Hale, "Focus and Scope of a School of Social Work," Journal of Education for Social Work, Vol. 3, No. 2 (Fall 1967), p. 39.

[5] Carl M. Shafer, "Teaching Social Work Practice in an Integrated

particular aspects of practice (knowledge, values, and methods) than to its whole scope, suggests a readiness to move toward a consideration of the common base of all practice, which is the next logical and urgently needed step for the profession.[6]

Another step before the profession, as stated earlier, is to deal with the limitations in its own thinking. In their practice, teaching, and writing, social workers have been influenced by ideas that are divisive rather than integrative. Furthermore, they have used ideas that are not necessarily opposites as if they were alternatives and as if choices must be made between them. Examples would be "cause and function," "generic and specific," "individual and community," and "person and environment." Such an approach may temporarily clarify specific entities in comparison with each other, but it tends to block movement toward broader concepts because of its divisive effect. In discussing some of the well-known intellectual controversies, such as "nature versus nurture" or the "body-mind" problem, Ausubel points out that as long as the interactional position is restricted to a general statement of bipolar determination, the hub of the controversy merely shifts from all-or-none propositions to conflicting estimates of overall relative importance. "The pseudo-issue underlying the controversy," he says, "can only be eliminated by specifying in more precise and detailed fashion how the interaction takes place and the relative weight of each factor in determining the course and outcome. . . ." [7]

Course: A General Systems Approach," in Gordon Hearn, ed., *The General Systems Approach: Contributions toward an Holistic Conception of Social Work* (New York: Council on Social Work Education, 1969), p. 26.

[6] *See* Herbert Aptekar's use of the term in his review of *Theory for Social Work Practice* by Ruth Elizabeth Smalley (New York: Columbia University Press, 1967), in the *Social Service Review*, Vol. 41, No. 3 (September 1967), pp. 342–344. Aptekar says: "If social work is indeed a single profession, as medicine may be said to be, it must have a common base, as medical practice does." His usage seems similar to the one in this monograph. (The writer does not, however, concur with him in his application of the term "generic" to social work practice, believing that it should be used to describe the underlying principles, not the practice itself.)

[7] David P. Ausubel, *Theory and Problems of Child Development* (New York: Grune & Stratton, 1958), p. 50. Ausubel says further: "When this approach is adopted, the irrelevancy of dichotomous or overall estimates becomes apparent, and we are left with a genuine scientific problem which

It is this bipolar approach that has persisted in social work in relation to the person-situation, person-environment concepts. The two variables have been viewed together as being social work's concern without the forging of a meaningful connection between them. Now if in analyzing social situations social workers would direct their attention to the nature of the exchange between people and environment, this would be a way of eliminating the bipolar thinking. The suggested concept of social functioning is such an interactional concept, which has the potential for overcoming many of the barriers presented by the divisive approach that has been so common in social work.

In examining social workers' perceptions of their practice, past and present, the writer became increasingly impressed with the need for stronger and clearer ideas regarding the profession's central focus. General statements about the nature of professions usually tie a profession's domain to its knowledge and competence, whereas social work's problem seems to start further back, in its difficulty in defining its area of central concern. Flexner implied this problem in 1915 when he concluded that social work was not yet a profession because it had not limited or defined its own area and its efforts were mainly directed toward supplementing the work of other professions.[8] In discussing comparative developments in social work, medicine, and law in 1943, Brown concluded that social work had made enormous strides in the preceding decade —not matched by the two other professions—but then asked why social work had "found itself in a relatively undistinguished position" during the war period.[9] This is, of course, the same question that has been posed more recently regarding the current era of social change.

The need for and value of integrative concepts to clarify the social work focus becomes increasingly urgent. Some social workers have identified one of social work's characteristics as that

---

can be formulated in terms of theoretical postulates that are both meaningful and empirically testable."

[8] Abraham Flexner, "Is Social Work a Profession?" *Proceedings of the National Conference of Charities and Correction* (Chicago: National Conference of Charities and Correction, 1915), pp. 576–590.

[9] Esther Lucile Brown, "Comparative Developments in Social Work, Medicine, and Law," *The Family*, Vol. 24, No. 7 (November 1943), pp. 254–255.

of being an integrative force in society; [10] but the step of producing the needed concepts to pull social work's own thinking and activities together has not been taken. It seems possible that the fragmentation in social work practice and the delay in knowledge-building may have been largely due to this lack of integrative ideas for identifying the profession's focus.

The emphasis on the skill of the individual practitioner—at an earlier period of social work history—contributed to the strength of social work as a helping profession. But this very concern with "feeling and doing," related to each other in a sensitive and disciplined manner, deflected attention from "thinking and knowing," the essential cognitive component in any professional practice. So also, while there was concern with the individual practitioner, his supervision and growth, there was not equal movement toward a comprehensive view of social work practice. Thus the relation between the practice of the individual social worker and the broad essentials of his profession's practice was not faced (except in a fragmented way in some of the fields). For its delay in bringing these aspects of its practice together social work was later to pay a heavy price in terms of its unreadiness to deal with the widening problems of a changing society.

Full recognition of the common base will mean, of course, that discussions of various aspects of social work and its practice—whether some phase of knowledge, an interventive approach, practice in a particular area, or some other aspect—will begin with the recognition that they rest on and derive their meaning from the common base of the profession. That is, the common base comes first because it is the essence of the profession, and the segments all take their place in relation to the common base. Formerly it was customary to discuss such segments independently, with only limited reference to their relation to practice as a whole. In the early sixties, influenced by the "Working Definition of Social Work Practice" and the Social Work Curriculum Study of the Council on Social Work Education, writers began emphasizing the common base underlying particular segments of practice. What

---

[10] Katherine A. Kendall, "Social Work Education in Review," *Social Service Review*, Vol. 24, No. 3 (September 1950), p. 299; and Alfred J. Kahn, "The Function of Social Work in the Modern World," in Kahn, ed., *Issues in American Social Work*, p. 26.

had previously been unexpressed was now articulated. Konopka placed group work clearly within social work; Schwartz also affirmed this relationship. In discussing school social work, Johnson described its base in social work practice. In analyzing and describing social work practice in the health field, this author made a special effort to show how the practice in a particular field rests upon the common base.[11] This kind of recognition of the relation between the whole practice and its parts will greatly consolidate the strengths of social work.

The idea that the various components of the common base (see diagram on page 130) guide the individual social worker in his practice brings together the two models of practice—the method-and-skill model and the professional model. Being thus fused, they can now form one overall model of the profession and its practice. The fragmentation of practice by fields, methods, and agency programs should diminish now that all such practice segments can be related to each other through the concept of their common base. Knowledge-building and the definition of professional competence—two essential steps that have lagged in social work—will be also clarified and stimulated.

Comprehensive and integrative ideas, such as the common base of social work practice, can have far-reaching impact on social workers' perceptions of their profession and its contribution in society. Such ideas often develop their own momentum. Even at an early stage of formulation—as can be seen in this discussion— such ideas can begin to counteract fragmented and divisive approaches that previously prevailed. Social workers too often have sought answers to their problems through single solutions. The profession needs to examine potentially useful clusters of theory, such as those of behavioral science, but this theory should be examined and tested within the profession's own value-knowledge

---

[11] Gisela Konopka, *Social Group Work: A Helping Process* (Englewood Cliffs, N.J.: Prentice-Hall, 1963); William Schwartz, "The Social Worker in the Group," *The Social Welfare Forum, 1961* (New York: Columbia University Press, 1961), pp. 146–171; Arlien Johnson, *School Social Work: Its Contribution to Professional Education* (New York: National Association of Social Workers, 1962); and Harriett M. Bartlett, *Social Work Practice in the Health Field* (New York: National Association of Social Workers, 1961).

frame of reference in a manner that previously was not possible.[12] Social work also needs innovative action in social change but such action should now be related to the profession's base so that it extends but does not destroy it.

Social workers have always been interested in exploring new ideas and new directions of action with freedom and individual initiative. Such freedom, an essential characteristic of scientific and professional thinking, has been a strength of social work but also, as has been shown, a liability, when it leads to fragmentation of action and diffusion of ideas. The proposed concept of social functioning, for instance, may be regarded by some social workers as restrictive. It is offered here as a broad and open-ended concept, in connection with which many related concepts and subconcepts can be developed. Certainly other directions of thinking should and will be explored. The ideas presented in this monograph are intended to clarify and free social workers' thinking, not to confine it. The emphasis is not on specific formulations but on finding comprehensive and integrative concepts, which will be useful and appropriate for social work at the same time that they stimulate its growth.

In order to bring out the strengths of social work, the definition of its common base should not only be integrative but also identify the distinctive contribution of this particular profession in society.[13] In now discussing some uses of the common base in practice, we shall give special consideration to the question of the social work contribution.

---

12 *See*, for example, Edwin J. Thomas, "Selected Sociobehavioral Techniques and Principles: An Approach to Interpersonal Helping," *Social Work*, Vol. 13, No. 1 (January 1968), pp. 12–26.

13 The NASW action in 1969 to broaden the membership will lead to a practice of increased scope and complexity. Thus the need to recognize the common base of social work practice becomes more urgent than ever before. Unless this base is established, the enlarged practice could become fragmented and diffuse, as happened in the early days. While the changes in membership require much administrative work to develop suitable structure and organization, equal effort is required to develop the social work foundation (knowledge, values, and interventive measures) on which the extended practice must rest if it is to be effective in producing better service.

part three
use of the
common base
in practice

9

professional judgment
in assessment

We have now arrived at a point where we have a clarified picture of social work practice within the outlines of the *professional* model. We have tried to define the social work focus on social functioning, the orientation to the people involved in the problem or situation, and the substance of the essential elements (value, knowledge, and interventive techniques). The next question is: How does this practice model become operational? How are the elements applied in practice? The Working Definition states that the essential elements guide the practitioner's action but does not take the next step of saying how this takes place. This we shall try to do at this point.

Professional Judgment

All professions rest on bodies of values and knowledge in the form of principles and generalizations. It is generally agreed that it is through the professional judgment and skill of the practitioner that they are applied. However, concepts of skill vary widely in social work. Some people would include the ability to use knowl-

139

edge effectively in performance, but this aspect has received little emphasis. In the writer's opinion, *professional judgment* is of such importance that it should receive greater recognition in its own right.[1]

Professional judgment is one of the most important features distinguishing occupations from professions. In occupations many activities can be routinely outlined so that workers can be given regular instructions about how to carry them out. Varying degrees of judgment and discretion are of course always necessary but not to the degree required in professional practice. In a profession the complexity and variability of the situations to be dealt with require the exercise of individual judgment by the practitioner in each new situation. Such judgment is a key operation in any profession. The practitioner must be able to select the relevant principles from his profession's body of knowledge and values and apply them appropriately in assessing the situation before him. While some writers who discuss criteria for professions, like Carr-Saunders and Wilson and Flexner, emphasize the importance of professional judgment, others do not.[2] In the author's view it must be stressed in any consideration of social work because social workers deal with complex, rapidly changing social situations and make decisions influencing the lives of many people in important ways. A high degree of responsibility is implied for which an equivalent degree of expertise and accountability are required.

---

[1] The expert judgments of social workers have been used in social work research. See Ann W. Shyne, ed., *Use of Judgments as Data in Social Work Research* (New York: National Association of Social Workers, 1959). Jack Stumpf refers to professional judgments as interventive acts in "Community Planning and Development," *Encyclopedia of Social Work* (New York: National Association of Social Workers, 1965), p. 194. In a working paper, the NASW Committee on the Study of Competence mentions one component of responsible, self-regulated practice as being the ability to "dependably exercise critical judgment in making wise decisions," a concept to be developed further as the committee's work proceeds. See "An Outline of Qualitative Components Relevant for Assessment of Professional Practice in Social Work" (New York: National Association of Social Workers, 1965), p. 1. (Mimeographed.)

[2] A. M. Carr-Saunders and P. A. Wilson, *The Professions* (Oxford, England: Clarendon Press, 1933); and Abraham Flexner, "Is Social Work a Profession?" *Proceedings of the National Conference of Charities and Correction* (Chicago: National Conference of Charities and Correction, 1915), pp. 576–590.

Features of Assessment in Social Work Practice

In this chapter we will consider the use of professional judgment by social workers in assessing social situations, which is the point at which judgment first comes into operation in practice. It is important to visualize and understand how such professional judgment is exercised in social work. We need to understand social workers' ways of assessing the full range of situations they face, whether in relation to individuals and families, groups of people, neighborhood services, community development, large governmental programs, or issues of national social policy. In today's expanding and changing practice, all social workers must be able to assess, at least in a preliminary way, a wide range of situations. This is one of the new challenges being presented to the profession.

Certain conditions are necessary for such a broadened use of professional judgment in assessment. (1) There must be some common concept of the profession's central focus, so that practitioners can think together in comprehensive terms. (2) Assessment must be consistently directed to an examination of the phenomena, conditions, and situations to be dealt with, since decisions regarding action and intervention must be based on understanding the problem. (3) A body of relevant propositions and generalizations, related through a growing system of theory, must be available to practitioners to guide them in their assessments.

These conditions, however, have not been present in social work practice. The method-and-skill model emphasized feeling and doing. Assessment as a distinct intellectual process, common to all social workers, has not been recognized and defined. "Diagnosis," as conceived in social work, has been customarily associated with and confined to a particular method and thus has been narrowly perceived. Developed first in casework and then in the other methods, it has followed the medical model, which is based on a classification of diseases and pathologies. Lacking a typology of problems in social work, however, social workers have defined many kinds of diagnosis, oriented toward causal factors, current dynamics, clinical categories, problem types and problem-solving, assessing and establishing objectives, and similar approaches.[3] The

---

[3] *See* Helen Harris Perlman, *Social Casework: A Problem-solving Process* (Chicago: University of Chicago Press, 1957), pp. 164–182; Florence

fact that social workers were using clusters of knowledge from separate sources, mainly about individuals, groups, and communities or agencies, programs, and settings, meant that this diagnostic thinking was still further fragmented.

Another important characteristic of social work practice has been that the diagnostic process was customarily shared with the people served and other associates, with conscious use of the professional relationship. This way of working with others developed from the social worker's respect for people and the recognition that the results of assessment are less effective when decisions are imposed upon others. Early in social work history, through psychiatric theory social workers became aware of the importance of using the professional relationship with the individual skillfully and responsibly because of the risk of developing emotional dependence rather than stimulating growth. Theory regarding group process extended these insights to small groups. More recently, there has been recognition of the forces operating to further or block the efforts of the professional worker to help larger groups assess their situations or to carry through joint thinking with professional planners and experts.[4]

Of further significance is the concept of "study, diagnosis, and treatment" as developed in social work. Although these can logically be considered as separate and sequential steps, in social work practice they were found to involve considerable overlapping. Here the use of the client-worker relationship in casework treatment was of particular importance. There was general agreement, as stated by Hamilton, that "treatment begins at the first

---

Hollis, *Casework: A Psychosocial Therapy* (New York: Random House, 1964), pp. 179–203; Gisela Konopka, *Social Group Work: A Helping Process* (Englewood Cliffs, N.J.: Prentice-Hall, 1963), pp. 79–106; and Meyer Schwartz, "The Problem of Defining Community Organization Practice," "Defining Community Organization Practice" (New York: National Association of Social Workers, 1962), pp. 15–17 (mimeographed).

[4] In a current examination of community organization, Arnold Gurin divides the professional tasks into two kinds, "analytical, or the rational treatment of the substantive problems involved; and interactional, or the interpersonal relationships that are involved in dealing with the problem." "The Community Organization Curriculum Development Project: A Preliminary Report," *Social Service Review*, Vol. 42, No. 4 (December 1968), p. 426.

contact." [5]   Thus the three parts of the casework method traditionally have been viewed in practice and taught in schools as
intertwined, simultaneous occurrences.[6]

Several results followed from these features of assessment as
it developed in social work practice. The concept of treatment
as beginning with the first contact moved practitioners into immediate action, not only in casework but also in other areas
of practice. The social worker's responsibility to analyze and
understand the situation with which he must deal *before* taking
action—an essential of all professional practice—was not fully
recognized. Emphasis on skill as feeling and doing and on sharing assessment with others in the situation prevented assessment
from standing out in its own right as an intellectual process based
on knowledge and value. Furthermore, because of the incorporation of diagnostic thinking within the three methods, assessment
was unnecessarily limited in scope. Thus the unintended consequences of these perceptions of social work practice were to retard
movement toward recognition of the use of professional judgment
in assessment as a distinct and basic process in social work
practice.

Assessment As a Cognitive Process

In its general outlines, professional assessment is a form of
logical analysis that would be carried through by any person with
a trained mind. It requires the kind of objective and rigorous
thinking characteristic of the scientific method. However, this
is not all. It is also a *social work* assessment and therefore must
demonstrate the characteristics of the profession's approach to
situations and problems. Since the common base of practice is
only partially defined, we are breaking new ground here in trying
to describe assessment in this way. But the attempt seems worthwhile because there is currently a gap in the practice model at
this point—between knowledge and value, on the one hand, and

[5] Gordon Hamilton, *Theory and Practice of Social Case Work* (New York: Columbia University Press, 1940), p. 166.

[6] Helen Harris Perlman, "Social Casework," *Encyclopedia of Social Work* (New York: National Association of Social Workers, 1965), p. 706.

their application in practice on the other hand—which needs to be filled. We shall consider first the general outlines of assessment as a cognitive process and then examine some of its social work characteristics.

The process of assessment can be viewed as covering the following steps: (1) analysis of the situation to identify the major factors that are operating in it; (2) identification of those factors that appear most critical, definition of their interrelationships, and selection of those to be dealt with; (3) consideration of possible alternatives for social work action, based on prediction of possible outcomes; and (4) decision as to the specific approach and action to be taken.[7]

Analysis. In facing any one of a wide variety of situations with which he may be concerned, the social worker must first analyze the situation to identify the major factors operating in it. The initial examination, known as the process of study, involves the use of observation, interviews, documents, and similar means. Various criteria to guide the collection of relevant data have been developed in the past in connection with the three methods. However, the situations can now be expected to be of wider scope and variety than previously dealt with because diagnosis can no longer be confined within a single method.

Interaction between people and environment, the area of social work's central concern, involves multiple factors—biological, psychological, social, economic, and others—all of which must be identified and related in assessing a single social situation. Concepts adequate in either clarity or breadth for enabling social workers to deal with so many variables in a systematic manner distinctive of their profession have not been available.

Another aspect, which has not received the recognition it deserves, is that such analysis requires rapid, continuous, expert selection and use of appropriate generalizations from the profes-

---

[7] Descriptions of assessment as a basic process in social work practice do not seem available in the literature. Boehm has described some of the steps under "Activities of Social Work." *See* Werner W. Boehm, *Objectives of the Social Work Curriculum of the Future* (New York: Council on Social Work Education, 1969), p. 53. *See also,* Gary A. Lloyd, "Integrated Methods and the Field Practice Course," *Social Work Education Reporter,* Vol. 16, No. 2 (June 1968), pp. 39–42.

sion's body of knowledge. It is because the selection must be so rapid that the knowledge must be visible and readily available to the practitioner. The wider the range of situations faced, the broader must be the knowledge. Social change in our society now requires that all social workers be able to operate flexibly and respond intelligently to the full range of social work's concern.

Identification of critical factors. The next step in assessment involves identifying the particular factors (from among those regarded as major in the situation) that appear most critical and defining their interrelationship. This is, of course, a key step in assessment and often must be repeated several times as understanding grows or situations change. The factors to be dealt with are then selected in terms of their significance in creating the problem or their probable response to social work interventive efforts. Just as a physician makes a prognosis in relation to the probable course of the disease in an individual case, so the social worker considers—as far as his knowledge permits—the ongoing course and possible trends in the social situation. Such analysis might, for instance, point most strongly to deficiency in coping capacity or deficiency in environmental supports or some combination of the two. According to the concept of social functioning, coping capacity and environmental demand can no longer be considered separately but always in interaction with each other.

Alternatives for action. In the third step, alternatives for social work action are considered and a prediction of their possible outcomes is made. This involves defining objectives and weighing the relevance and feasibility of various alternative lines of action. The social worker may decide that all or part of the situation does not belong to social work. If it is within social work's scope, then he must decide which aspects are likely to be most responsive to social work's interventive approaches and why. Note that what is involved is not a "group worker" assessing a "group work problem" but a *social worker* scanning the profession's full interventive repertoire.

Deciding what action to take. The final step in assessment is that of deciding on the specific approach and action to be taken. The social worker may decide that some combination of interventive approaches is needed, such as direct help to families combined with neighborhood services. As a social worker, he will have competence in at least one type of intervention and if he is an experienced worker, probably at least initial competence in several others. If the situation he faces is in an early stage of development, he may decide to offer consultation at first, with the aim of drawing in other social workers possessing the necessary competence at a later date.

Having made the necessary decisions, the social worker moves into the action to which this whole process of assessment has been directed. The assessment may be telescoped into a brief period or greatly extended. As has been pointed out, it is shared with others in the situation and interwoven with interventive action as situations evolve. In social work, as in other professions, assessment can only be effective if it is recognized by the practitioner as a conscious intellectual process, to be carried on deliberately, responsibly, and expertly.

Professional Foundation for Assessment

We can now see why the efforts in preceding chapters to define and describe the profession's focus and primary orientation, along with its process of knowledge-building, are relevant for the use of professional judgment in assessment. It seems probable that the quality of assessment required to deal with the complex problems of today's society can only be attained when the conditions for its operation are built into the professional base.

Stages in Assessment

The whole purpose of assessment is to enable social workers to gain sufficient understanding so that they can bring about social change effectively in particular situations which confront them as *social workers*. This requires a well-grounded definition of the social work contribution in each situation. Three stages of assessment that are of particular importance in this ongoing intellectual process are concerned with the following: (1) the common base of social work practice, (2) viewing social situations, and (3) the decision regarding social work intervention.[8] These approaches to social work practice were first developed by the writer in connection with an analysis of practice in specific fields.[9] They have influenced the total thinking in this monograph and will be used at this point to discuss social work assessment.

The diagram on page 148 suggests the main outlines of these stages in assessment and their relation to each other. The suggested stages do not cover all the essential steps in assessment. They have been selected because they appear to be of special importance as social work practice moves from the traditional diagnosis within particular methods toward the broader type of assessment now required.

In order to understand how such professional guides to assessment may operate, we will assume that they are being used by experienced social workers, aware of the full scope of social work practice and possessing mastery of its essentials. These social workers are not confined to operating in terms of any particular agency or field but are guided primarily by professional principles. From this position they are prepared to view the wide range of situations with which they and their profession must deal.

Starting Point: The Common Base

The first stage covers the *common base of social work practice,* which now includes not only the essential elements (values, knowledge, and interventive techniques) as identified in the "Working Definition of Social Work Practice," but also the focus on social functioning and the orientation toward the people with the problem, as developed in Chapters 6 and 7. The assumption is that all social workers will start from this common base in making assessments. This is, in fact, what makes them social workers.

---

[8] Here *stage* is taken to mean "a period or step in a process, activity, or development." *See Webster's Third New International Dictionary* (Springfield, Mass.: G. & C. Merriam Co., 1961), p. 2219.

[9] Harriett M. Bartlett, *Analyzing Social Work Practice by Fields* (New York: National Association of Social Workers, 1961), pp. 18–19.

FIGURE 3. STAGES IN ASSESSMENT OF SOCIAL SITUATIONS

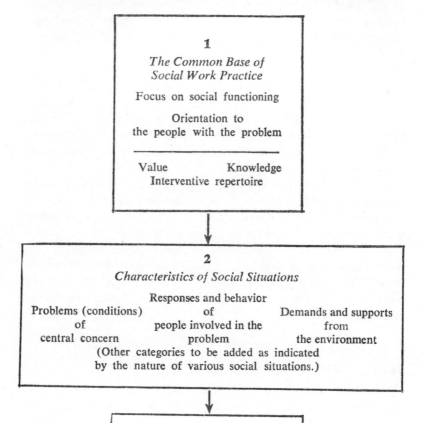

1

*The Common Base of
Social Work Practice*

Focus on social functioning

Orientation to
the people with the problem

Value   Knowledge
Interventive repertoire

2

Characteristics of Social Situations

Responses and behavior

Problems (conditions)   of   Demands and supports
of   people involved in the   from
central concern   problem   the environment
(Other categories to be added as indicated
by the nature of various social situations.)

3

Use of
the Common Base
of Social Work Practice
for
Assessment of Social Situations
Leading to
Decisions on
Interventive Action

Guided by such perceptions, all social workers should now be able to start from this base in assessing social situations and move toward the more specific, specialized, and partial aspects of their practice relevant to the situations they face. This is, in one sense, a reversal of the traditional social work approach which so emphasized the uniqueness of each individual or situation and the methodological differences that it provided no effective way for social workers to identify what was common in their practice.

With progress toward a common base, social workers need no longer operate with so many hidden assumptions regarding their practice. They can more readily perceive and use what is common and what is specific in relation to each other. However, such fundamental changes in perceptions take time. Until such time as all social workers recognize the common elements in practice and operate easily and naturally on the common base, we must keep reminding ourselves that assessment starts consciously and deliberately from this base.

Viewing Social Situations from the Social Work Base

A second stage covers the *characteristics of social situations* as viewed from the common base of social work practice. This is taken to mean viewing and seeking to understand specific social situations *before* there is substantial social work intervention or effort to change the situation. The way that social workers view specific situations with which they must deal obviously represents a crucial step from the common base toward the decision regarding interventive action. The word "situation" is used here in the sense of a particular complex of affairs or circumstances that confronts one social worker, a group of social workers, or the whole profession and must be assessed by them. It is used to cover the full range of such circumstances, from the individual to the whole field of practice.[10] The attempt to consider within one perspective the full range of situations with which social

---

[10] At this period in the development of social work practice, it seems preferable to use a general term like *situation* without any effort to give it a distinctive social work meaning. A term is needed that will cover practice without fragmenting it. *See* Werner W. Boehm, "Toward New Models of Social Work Practice," *Social Work Practice, 1967* (New York: Colum-

workers are concerned is new and unfamiliar. However, it must be attempted because the need for such an advance is urgent.

Basic concepts. The basic concepts of social work guide the practitioner's initial view of social situations, as is shown in the diagram on page 148. The primary social work orientation toward people and their needs leads to the question: What people are involved here? Are we concerned with individuals and families in their relationships with others? with small groups of people in neighborhoods? with large population groups? If the social worker is a social planner dealing with agencies and programs, he must still ask what people they are serving. The next question relates to the needs of the people, that is: What problem or condition is central in this situation? Is there one major problem such as health or the provision of community services? Or is there a complex of undefined, interrelated problems?

Social situations do not in themselves reveal which of their characteristics are important for social workers. Lacking a clear concept of the profession's focus in the past, social workers had to use such guides for assessment as were available in the various segments of practice. That is why integrative concepts, such as that of social functioning, are now so important. Following this concept, basic questions can be asked regarding the responses of the people in the situation. What is the impact of the situation on them? What is its meaning to them? How are they coping with it? At the same time that the people's responses are being considered, the demands and supports of the environment are also being examined. What are the positive opportunities for people in the community? What are the most serious limitations? What social groups and institutions are dominant and how do they operate? What agencies, programs, and services are involved? What knowledge and techniques, what economic resources are available to deal with the situation? What sociocultural attitudes are of particular significance? The concept of social functioning

---

bia University Press, 1967), pp. 3–18, in which he suggests a somewhat similar but more restricted use of the concept of situation. One distinction in terminology is to be noted. These are specific situations with which social workers deal in their daily work, usually called "cases" or "problems." They are to be distinguished from the "life situations" associated with the concepts of task and coping discussed in Chapter 6.

leads to a disciplined analysis of all these factors through an examination of the coping patterns of the people, the demands and supports of the environment, the exchanges between people and environment, and the resulting balance or imbalance. The diagram on page 148 can only show some of the major concepts for guiding assessment during this stage. Additional questions and concepts relevant for particular situations will be needed and will have to be developed by practitioners and researchers as the actual use of assessment in practice is examined and clarified.

Through the use of professional judgment in assessing situations with which he must deal, the practitioner puts his professional knowledge to its first important use. The visibility and availability of relevant knowledge are crucial for social work practice. The fact that the profession must have a broad and growing body of knowledge does not mean that all practitioners must encompass the whole mass of knowledge. That would be impossible. It does mean that they must command the major generalizations and theoretical propositions so that they will be able to find what is relevant for their use at any one time. Theory regarding separation and alienation is already recognized and being applied in this way. Theory regarding crisis is in the process of being worked out within the practice of social work and other professions. In order not to be dependent on a single cluster of knowledge or a few familiar theories, as has happened in the past, social workers will need to master a larger number of key propositions, which are still to be identified by the profession.

Clues for selecting knowledge. Basic theory is not enough; the practitioner also needs clearer guides for selecting knowledge in relation to his practice. Consider the two clusters of knowledge traditionally used in social work and known as "sequences" in the educational curriculum. They relate to (1) human behavior and the social environment and (2) social welfare policy and services. The need for social workers to have knowledge about man—particularly about the physical organism and its development, the personality, and the culture—is only too clear. The same is true in relation to social welfare, in which knowledge about social institutions and social policy is especially important.

However, ideas that would bring these two kinds of knowledge together in a meaningful way were too long hidden in social work's own practice, within the methods and fields of practice.

Because the cognitive aspect of assessment was not emphasized in its own right and was so often embedded in the helping process itself, practitioners have not been sufficiently aware of the knowledge they use in practice. They need to be familiar not only with a considerable number of theoretical propositions but also with clues to selecting those most relevant to the specific situation they confront. One important characteristic and strength of social work, previously mentioned, has been that in viewing situations social workers have not usually thought in terms of single causes but have viewed social situations as involving interaction of multiple factors. They have also sought and used many kinds of knowledge and theory. This has, however, been done unevenly—by different groups and at different times—and often ineffectively because the profession did not provide practitioners with comprehensive guides for selecting appropriate knowledge propositions and applying them consistently in practice.

These needed concepts and criteria to guide the social worker's use of knowledge come first from the core of the profession. A comprehensive concept concerned with people interacting and coping with their environment gives promise of offering a central focus and a group of related subconcepts adequate to provide the necessary guidance. Here are to be found the ideas relating to life tasks, coping patterns, environmental demands and supports, exchanges between people and their environment, and new concepts not yet perceived, all of which require disciplined examination and testing by the profession.

Practitioners must be able to judge when knowledge used by all social workers—that which is common for the profession—is sufficient to guide them in assessing situations and when additional knowledge is needed. Social workers practicing regularly in the health field must command a larger body of concepts and theory regarding health and disease, psychosocial aspects of illness, and essentials of medical care than other social workers. Similarly, other social workers concerned with specific social problems and services must master the theory related to their practice. Because of the wide range of problems and the need to understand their meaning to people, social workers must be equipped to use special as well as basic knowledge in assessment. Especially in times of rapid change, social workers need guides in the form of concepts and criteria about how to select, try out, combine, and apply the various kinds of knowledge they must use in assessment.

Decisions Regarding Social Work Intervention

A third stage of assessment (also in the diagram on page 148) relates to use of the common base in reaching decisions regarding social work intervention. This is a situation into which the social worker and his profession, as represented by him, are about to become involved. His purpose is to define the kind of social change needed and what social workers can do, through their distinctive approach and expertise, to influence movement toward this change. Some of the first steps will be considered here; the discussion will be carried on in the next chapter.

Out of the multiple factors discovered in the broad preliminary view, the practitioner must identify those that appear most critical and define their interrelationship. In this stage of assessment, the concept of social functioning continues to guide the practitioner because it covers not only the active interchange between people and their environment but also the consequences of such exchange. The practitioner will have to consider the various consequences that can be regarded as possibly ensuing from the social situation and determine which interventive approaches may be most effective in dealing with them. Social work values, as they relate to people and environment, will be continually taken into account in these decisions regarding action.

At this point another segment of social work knowledge becomes relevant, that relating to the range of interventive actions the profession can offer at any one time. Here again we are breaking new ground because social workers have traditionally directed their thinking along one track or another in considering the interventive measures to be applied in a specific situation. It is clear that the profession must now bring together the knowledge which all practitioners should have regarding the range of interventive approaches in social work. This knowledge should be viewed more as ways of influencing social change in people or institutions than as skills to be learned. Thus, in assessment every social worker will be able to consider the alternative measures of intervention his profession can offer. His decision about the action needed in specific situations will then be determined not narrowly in terms of his own particular competence or his agency's program but broadly in terms of his profession's full interventive repertoire.

As integrated and focused knowledge regarding social functioning is developed and included in the profession's system of knowledge, it can be anticipated that assessment strengthened by such knowledge will lead to more effective intervention in social situations. A practitioner who views situations in terms of patterns of coping and environmental demands and who commands growing knowledge about the relation between them will be in a position to influence change in a manner not possible before. Ways in which aged people can be offered opportunities to show interest in others who are deprived and thus enrich their own lives or professional workers in multiservice centers can listen more fully and respond more effectively to what people are trying to say to them would be examples of such exchanges. When common patterns are observed, recognized, and tested, social workers will have clues to ways of working with people and their environment which may be immediately effective, so that the people can soon carry on by themselves. This approach suggests a broader scope for short-term service than has yet been visualized, through increased and better focused knowledge.

Since this discussion is concerned with the common characteristics of social work assessment, no attempt has been made to consider the various diagnostic approaches now being used in social work practice. One point, however, is clear. As long as these approaches are used separately, they continue to fragment practice. Just as the specific knowledge used by different groups of practitioners needs to be continually related to the common base of knowledge, so the various diagnostic approaches (types of professional assessment) are based on and should be kept in continual relation to the profession's common base.

Instances from Practice

The concept of assessment as a cognitive process and the stages in assessment proposed here cannot be fully demonstrated in today's practice, but instances from practice illustrate trends in this direction. Consider the school situation reported by Vinter and Sarri. This study was concerned with the malperformance of children in school and involved innovations in practice, concepts, and research design.[11] We are particularly interested in what it shows us regarding social work ways of *viewing and assessing social situations.*

The concept guiding the examination in this study was that "malperformance patterns should be viewed as *resultants of the interaction of both pupil characteristics and school conditions."* [12] Most malperforming pupils in the study group were found to have the innate capability to achieve satisfactorily. Nevertheless the large majority were performing below their capabilities and also manifesting various behavioral problems. Schools used a variety of negative sanctions to curb malperformance. Each school's system produced somewhat different kinds of pupils and problem behavior. Children who performed below a certain standard received low grades and might also be denied a wide variety of privileges and opportunities within the school. They lost esteem among their classmates and were often subjected to negative parental responses. Since the schools' record systems documented malperformance in detail, it was hard for the student to live down his past. Teachers regarded student motivation as crucial and considered the penalty system necessary to mobilize pupil concern. They were also concerned about maintaining desirable conditions within the classroom and effective control over their students. In some schools, malperforming children were perceived to be challenging the teachers' authority.

The children were aware of the school system and felt burdened by their negative history. "When you get in trouble, they never let up on you," said one child. An important finding was that most of these children were deficient in social skills needed for positive relations in the classroom. They suffered from self-doubt and suspicion that they were being singled out by their teachers. As a result, minor incidents often escalated into major crises. The findings show poor communication and excessive demands by the school in relation to the children's coping capacities.

---

[11] Robert D. Vinter and Rosemary C. Sarri, "Malperformance in the Public School: A Group Work Approach," *Social Work,* Vol. 10, No. 1 (January 1965), pp. 3–13. This article was reprinted in Edwin J. Thomas, ed., *Behavioral Science for Social Workers* (New York: Free Press, 1967), pp. 350–362.

[12] *Ibid.,* p. 4.

This is an instance of social work assessment of the character discussed earlier in this chapter. Although undertaken by group workers, it is not a diagnosis within a single method but a broad assessment of the situation. The factors emphasized as critical are those that are major to the concept of social functioning proposed in this monograph, namely, children coping with the demands of the school environment and the kind of exchange taking place between children and the school. This is an interactional view which, in its application in this situation, revealed that the school may maintain and even generate the very malperformance it seeks to eliminate.[13]

Since this was a research project, examination of the situation (study and assessment) had to be undertaken before action. Clear definition of concepts was also necessary as a basis for formulating hypotheses. We thus see demonstrated the value of broad assessment, based on concepts appropriate for social work, as the first step in dealing with a complex social situation. It is this quality and scope of assessment that needs to be recognized and applied in all professional social work practice today.

The second aspect of this project that interests us is the *definition of interventive action*. On the basis of the assessment and preliminary findings it revealed, group workers worked with groups of children as part of the project. Emphasis was on mobilizing a desire for improved achievement and on learning skills for coping more effectively with stressful school experiences. Group workers also maintained frequent contact with teachers and the school staff to interchange views and in the effort to modify perceptions and practice toward malperforming pupils on the part of school personnel. According to the teachers' ratings before and after group work service, the children in the service groups, as compared with controls, showed significant improvement, particularly in the areas of classroom conduct and academic motivation and performance.

Because this is a study, there is the advantage of a later redefinition of the interventive approach, based on the findings and experience, which is not customary in daily practice. This evaluation was done at a time when the study was not yet completed

---

[13] Walter E. Schafer, "Deviance in the Public School: An Interactional View," in Thomas, ed., *op. cit.*, pp. 57–58.

but some general review was possible. The implications for a modified interventive approach for social work are stated as follows:

> Because of their close acquaintance with malperforming pupils, and their knowledge of the conditions which impinge on these pupils, social workers in schools occupy a strategic location. They have the opportunity to assist teachers and administrators in identifying those school practices and arrangements that inadvertently contribute to malperformance, and that curtail learning and adjustment. . . . If the social worker concentrates his energies mainly on helping *some* pupils accommodate to the school, he can do little to ameliorate the patterns that will continue to generate difficulties for many *other* students. If he addresses himself primarily to attributes of the pupil (or his family situation) which seem to be contributing to malperformance, the effectiveness of his helping efforts will be greatly reduced. It seems important, therefore, that the social worker retain dual perspectives, and attempt to resolve problem *situations* or *processes;* both pupils and school conditions should be targets of his interventive activity.[14]

From this instance we see the importance of the social work way of viewing social situations and its impact on decisions regarding intervention. The interactional concept on which the project was based related children and school (people and environment) in a manner characteristic of social work. The resulting assessment led to a broader definition of social work responsibilities and enlarged opportunities for interventive action.

A second instance shows the kind of assessment involved when traditional social work seeks innovative approaches to the new and urgent problems of social change. It deals with a Youth Service Project developed by a family agency in a medium-sized community, in response to the needs of ghetto residents.[15] Although presented as an agency report, the material reveals the central role and contribution of the professional social workers in planning and action.

---

[14] Vinter and Sarri, *op. cit.,* p. 362.
[15] Salvatore Ambrosino, "A Family Agency Reaches Out to a Slum Ghetto," *Social Work,* Vol. 11, No. 4 (October 1966), pp. 17–23.

Throughout the project there was "a constant effort to refine a conceptual framework that establishes the priority of problems and guides the organization of services in the most effective manner." Study of the situation revealed severe "deficiencies that result from cultural, social, and economic deprivation," leading to underdevelopment and progressive helplessness. The children were not "vitally connected to life." A range of services to deal with three main emphases was designed.

The first emphasis was placed on offering opportunities to children and young people for education, employment, and social advancement. One example was a "verbal interaction project" based on experiments in working with culturally deprived pre-school children. It is found that the disadvantaged mother generally talks infrequently to her young child and does not know how to play with him. Therefore, caseworkers visited the home to demonstrate the use of selected toys, games, and books to the mother and child and reviewed materials in subsequent visits.

The second emphasis was in the area of neighborhood action. A group of parents and teen-agers was formed to spotlight social problems and obtain remedial action with the assistance of appropriate resources. The group learned to present issues, procedures for negotiation, and the power it had to influence community officials.

A third emphasis was in the area of community development. A broad-based committee of influential citizens was formed to deal with a critical community problem—a rapidly changing section that threatened to become another ghetto.

The small professional staff of the family agency participated in the planning process. They did not regard their work as an adjunctive service, as is common in community centers. In the projects their work was merged with that of many others, including teachers, aides, and volunteers.

The continuity of the program has been sufficient to permit evaluation of preliminary results. Children in the projects showed educational gains along with social and emotional growth. The action group sparked neighborhood improvements. The community development effort spread from the local area into the surrounding county. In spite of many problems in offering service, positive results were thus evident.

Social workers are increasingly being called upon to assess

situations such as this, which encompass whole population groups. In this instance, while assessment as a separate process is not fully discussed, it is clear that problems were defined and conceptualized before action was planned and that the action taken rested on a choice, from among a range of alternatives, of those that seemed to have the greatest potential for influencing the problems as defined. We need more reports such as this, with fuller discussion of the steps in assessment, so that we can understand better how social workers go about the assessment of such extensive, diffuse, and urgent social situations.

Assessment As a Basic Professional Process

The major points made in this chapter about assessment are as follows:

1. Professional judgment provides a bridge between knowledge and value, on the one hand, and interventive action, on the other. Assessment is its first application in practice.

2. Competence in the assessment of complex situations is a major characteristic of mature professions; it distinguishes them from occupations. In professional practice understanding precedes action.

3. Assessment is carried out within the frame of reference of each profession, using its particular resources of knowledge, value, and technique. Thus social work assessment rests on the common base of social work practice.

In assessment the predominant absorbing purpose is to _understand and identify._ This is not the usual pattern in social work, in which the prevailing conceptualization has pushed thinking toward planning and doing, toward interventive action. It is part of the hypothesis about a maturing profession, on which this monograph rests, that what social workers know and understand about people and their problems has not received the recognition it deserves and will become increasingly important in our changing society. Therefore, in the concept of assessment presented here the social worker focuses on trying to understand the situation before him; he analyzes and conceptualizes what he observes in social work terms. On this basis he defines his potential contribution. And only then, after a rigorous effort to understand, is he ready to plan and act.

In their analysis of social planning, Zweig and Morris make the same point when they emphasize that the social worker "initially explores the nature of the problem at issue, that he does not permit consideration of what to do about the problem to interfere with his full assessment of it, and that he frees his observational capacities to the greatest possible extent." [16] Insofar as the specific situation requires, the social worker must also be developing his professional working relationship with clients and others and meeting emergency needs as indicated. But the important point is that he does not allow these phases of his action as a social worker to divert him from the essential process of assessment. This approach places knowledge and value first; a decision on interventive action is arrived at only after assessment. It really puts the Working Definition into operation.

The view of study, diagnosis, and treatment as overlapping processes is no longer so useful as in the past and becomes confusing when applied to social work practice as a whole. Such a pattern was understandable at an earlier stage of practice when the knowledge available to social workers was limited. Direct methods of helping, which the social worker could offer at once through his own skill and action, seemed indicated. Now, however, social work presents problems of increasing scope and complexity. More knowledge is becoming available and it is recognized that intervention must rest on a solid base of knowledge. This means that, as in all professions, understanding must come before action, assessment before intervention. This in turn means giving a place to assessment as the initial major step in social work practice and postponing any substantial action or intervention (except in emergencies) until adequate understanding of the situation has been attained.

The implications of sharing the assessment with other associates and with persons who are being served, within the context of the professional relationship, will need to be re-examined by practitioners and teachers. Meanwhile, the cognitive aspects of assessment, as carried through by the practitioner himself, call for full recognition, examination, and description by the profession as an urgently needed step for strengthening practice.

[16] Franklin M. Zweig and Robert Morris, "The Social Planning Design Guide: Process and Proposal," *Social Work,* Vol. 11, No. 2 (April 1966), p. 14.

10

interventive action

In discussing assessment in the previous chapter, it was suggested that once the common base of the profession is established, all social workers will operate on this foundation. The common values, knowledge, and interventive techniques, along with the professional focus and orientation to people, will provide the base for assessing situations and will also guide the wide range of actions in practice.

In this chapter we shall examine how this process may take place. Because the elements are not sufficiently defined, the complexities of practice enormous, and practice in too great a state of flux, it is not possible at this time to show the use of the common base. This will be, therefore, a selective exploration with a view to understanding in a preliminary way how practice may appear through this approach.[1]

Our examination of practice suggests that social work is moving

---

[1] The reader is reminded that this is not a survey of practice but, particularly in this chapter, an analysis of social workers' thinking about their practice, based on the writer's experience in practice and education, examination of trends in professional thinking, and continuous interchange of ideas with many others in the profession. It is not intended as an inclusive or definitive statement but to point directions for further thinking.

and can continue to move toward developing a distinctive contribution as a profession which rests upon the common base of its practice as follows:

The beginning is in *social workers' ways of perceiving social situations,* which take into account *the coping efforts of people to deal with life tasks and problems as related to the demands of their environment and the consequences to both if there is a serious imbalance.* This is the emerging concept of *social functioning.* It is a strongly integrative concept that, as Hamilton says, always encompasses "the two ends of the psychosocial event," people and the environment.[2]

Next comes a *responsible assessment of the situation* in order to identify those factors within it with which social work is primarily concerned. This assessment rests on the common base of social work practice and requires the *exercise of professional judgment in using relevant values and knowledge* to arrive at such an analysis. The interventive measures are not considered or selected until the analysis of the situation has been made.

Such assessment provides the necessary preparation for moving into the *interventive action* itself, which is thus guided by a definition of the situation in terms of social work's own focus on people coping with their environment and by understanding the situation in terms of relevant knowledge and values. In interventive action, some social workers will place greater emphasis on giving direct services to the people coping with problems and others will emphasize bringing about changes in the social environment (including social institutions), but all must be continually aware of and concerned with the people and their environment in interaction with each other because this is the nature of social work.

A Practice Example

To understand better how the transition is taking place from the old method-and-skill model to the comprehensive professional

---

[2] Gordon Hamilton, "The Role of Social Casework in Social Policy," in Cora Kasius, ed., *Social Casework in the Fifties* (New York: Family Service Association of America, 1962), p. 33.

model of practice—from fragmented practice to a common base—at this point we present and discuss a practice example from the professional literature. Sometimes such practice examples, when selected and interpreted, seem larger than life and unrelated to everyday practice. A particular value of this example is that it shows a social worker—during a transitional period in the profession's development—moving step by step toward a more comprehensive concept of her professional practice and in this process taking the same steps that the profession is taking and must take. All the elements in the common base are implicit in this situation, which was that of a hospital ward in the Brooklyn, New York, Veterans Administration hospital, as reported by Foster.[3]

This was a ward on which patients with fatal blood diseases were treated. The forty patients were predominantly married men in early middle age. The procedure on this ward followed the traditional medical viewpoint that patients should be protected from unnecessary emotional pain. The assumption was that the doctor knows what is best for the patient and that other staff members, as well as patients and their families, should carry out the doctor's prescription, as they do in other areas of treatment. The ward physicians developed a stereotyped mode of behavior. They suppressed patients' questions about their condition and gave direct reassurance in response to patients' doubts. Families were given the responsibility of sharing what was regarded as a secret diagnosis with the physician. Patients were not encouraged to express their feelings and families were not given help with their ambivalence. Thus a "ward culture" had been established in which all played their appropriate roles.

Then a new social worker was assigned to the ward. In working with the men in the veterans hospital, the social worker found questions arising regarding the effects of the ward system. It was clear that the ward system solidified the defenses that most people under stress try to adopt, but the cost to and strain on the individuals involved were too great. As the worker explored the inner world of the patients, she found that they described feelings

---

[3] Zelda P. Leader Foster, "How Social Work Can Influence Hospital Management of Fatal Illness," *Social Work,* Vol. 10, No. 4 (October 1965), pp. 30–35.

of rejection, isolation, and abandonment. Even reactions of disturbing fantasies, despair, and hopelessness emerged. Direct reassurance had not dispelled underlying anxiety but aroused the patients' suspicion and distrust. Estrangement from families was also common. Patients complained that they were not allowed to participate in family decisions, as in the past, and that their families appeared upset and their reactions seemed artificial.

The social worker tried to utilize individual approaches in meeting the problem but found that these alone were not sufficient. It would also be necessary to intervene in the ward culture, particularly in the communication between doctors and patients. When the social worker, as a first step, shared the patients' feelings with the medical staff, the physicians denied these reactions or attributed them to the casework exploration itself. At this point, the social worker was able to demonstrate the need for change through three patients who wanted to know their prognosis because of their responsibility for future planning and proved that they could handle this knowledge directly and constructively to meet what lay ahead for themselves and for those close to them. These patients were also able to help other patients on the ward with their attitudes. The doctors observed how their own communication with patients and families improved. Thus the first steps were taken toward modifying the ward milieu.

At this hospital it was customary to hold weekly ward rounds for the resident physicians on the medical service to discuss the patients' social and adjustment problems and to work out plans for meeting them. Since residents changed every three months, this provided a way of introducing them to the new ward approach to patients and discussing the problems related to it.

It was a year before the situation really began to show signs of change. From then on, the new approach gradually became accepted and established on the ward. The majority of the ward patients were considered capable of understanding the nature of their diseases. Others in the situation, such as long-term and readmitted patients and the nursing staff, helped the social worker maintain the new ward culture. The social worker continued to work at developing and sustaining the project for four years.[4]

---

[4] *Ibid.*, supplemented by personal communications from the social service director and Mrs. Foster.

In her *way of perceiving the situation,* the social worker started from a casework base and moved toward a broader perception. Through working with individual patients she became aware that they were disturbed and anxious and had needs that were not being met. Seeking the causes, she found them in the ward milieu and the system that had been established to deal with the problem of fatal illness. It was evident that the coping capacities of the patients and families were inadequate for dealing with the demands being placed on them by the environment. Thus she realized that to be helpful to these individuals as a social worker, she would have to be concerned with the pattern of exchange—or lack of exchange—between the patients and the medical and nursing staffs of the ward, which had developed as a result of this system.

In her *assessment of the situation,* the social worker moved through several stages of analysis. In first giving casework service to the patients, she used her knowledge of ego psychology, particularly as related to defensive behavior and the capacity to deal with stress. Casework emphasizes individualization, that is, what is different among people. The social worker looked at the whole situation and perceived that these patients had a common problem which must be met. They and their families had a task to accomplish, a task so fundamental that it overshadowed all other considerations. The ward environment, instead of helping, was putting up a barrier to their coping efforts. Questions regarding values then arose. The social worker was keenly aware of the emotional pain involved in facing the problem of fatal illness but also was convinced that no helping profession had the responsibility or right to take away the individual's right to decide matters so deeply affecting his own life. The social worker asked herself: How far are social workers as well as physicians being influenced by avoidance of the kind of open, deep discussion and sharing of feeling that is painful? Can the helping professions decide for other people? Can they spare people pain? [5] Combining her knowledge and values, the social worker decided that she should intervene in the ward system while continuing to work with the patients and their families.

---

[5] Personal communication from Mrs. Foster.

In her description of her work, the social worker shows how she moved from a narrower to a broader perception of the situation and thus to a reassessment of the factors to be dealt with. As social work moves toward a common base, social workers can be expected to perceive and assess situations more broadly in this way, with greater awareness of the person-in-environment concept.

In moving into *interventive action,* the social worker combined direct service with other approaches, such as interprofessional teamwork and consultation. When she found that casework alone would not solve the problem, she did not at once turn to another method—as is frequently done in social work practice— but used her professional knowledge and judgment to reassess the situation and thus identified new factors to be dealt with. Neither did she confine herself to one cluster of knowledge. She testifies to the assistance received from group work consultants, who were at that time co-operating with the social service department, in conceptualizing the social system of the hospital and its impact on the patients.[6]

The social worker's primary orientation clearly was toward the patients, both as individuals and as a group of people facing a deeply traumatic problem. On such a medical ward, the closeness to the patients and the sense of sharing the problem with them are strong, since the social worker not only works with one individual after another but is daily moving among the whole group on the ward observing their behavior and constantly being aware of the difficulties they face as well as their anxiety. As often happens when the social work prediction of behavior is valid, several of the patients themselves demonstrated to the physicians their need to know their prognosis fully and their readiness to deal with the problems involved.[7] Social workers do not bring about such changes in complex social situations by a single limited action within the compass of a few weeks or months. For this social worker, it meant steady daily effort in working with patients, families, and the ward personnel. Progress had to be measured

---

[6] *Ibid.*
[7] It was recognized that there are some patients who could not deal directly with the reality of fatal illness and that further study would be needed to learn how to give them the necessary support and how best to meet their needs.

in years. Furthermore, the social worker could not accomplish this alone. Many patients, physicians, and nurses made their contribution to the change. It was the way in which the social worker's initial effort spread to the others concerned that brought positive results. It should also be noted that in the ward change was brought about in such a way that it was helpful to the doctors as well as the patients and families. In participating in this project, many physicians, who had not been been prepared by their medical education to deal with problems of this kind, went through considerable emotional stress but also acquired insights important for their own future work.

This example of social work practice shows the kind of help that can be given and the change that can be effected when social functioning is viewed as people coping with their social environment and social work intervention is directed at the intervening factors in such a situation, which have been identified through careful assessment. The concept of social functioning is implicit here; formal articulation will have to wait for greater recognition and clarification by the profession. The essential steps in use of the common base—viewing the situation as social functioning, assessment of the situation through relevant knowledge and values, and interventive action based on such perception and assessment—as demonstrated in this single instance of practice are applicable to the full range of practice, from work with an individual to problems affecting whole populations. In such practice the distinctive contribution of social work to society begins to take shape.

Use of Knowledge and Values

It is the thesis of this discussion that in order to have a significant impact on society, social workers must and should *operate on a strong, consistent common base*. It is probably because the limitations of social work practice have become so evident in recent years and many of its potential strengths, being hidden, have gone unrecognized, that so many social workers have turned away from their profession when they sought resources to meet the urgent problems of society. However, in moving into such diverse innovative actions and seeking new knowledge and strategy from outside sources—without bringing them together on some strong common foundation—are social workers in danger of repeating the patterns of past action that have kept social work practice fragmented and weakened its efforts? Could the profession's strengths thus be diluted and dissipated at the very time when they appear to be emerging with promise?

Suppose that the social workers faced with these urgent problems in our society and in our communities were to look to their profession to see what resources it had to offer. For example, in September 1967, Mitchell I. Ginsberg, chairman of the NASW Division of Social Policy and Action, and Daniel Thursz, chairman of the NASW Commission on Social Action, testified before the U.S. Senate Finance Committee on the House-passed social security amendments of 1967 (HR 12080). Under consideration were some controversial provisions relating to the AFDC (Aid to Families with Dependent Children) program that would require mothers to have job training and go to work and would place a ceiling on AFDC payments after a certain date, even if the number of children in need increased beyond that limitation. In regard to public assistance in general and these specific provisions, Ginsberg and Thursz testified as follows:

> The public assistance program was designed to provide basic financial support for the destitute, as well as services to encourage self-support where possible. On both counts, it has clearly not succeeded. Support payments in most states are too low to sustain even a minimal, decent standard of living; the method by which these payments are delivered encourages feelings of worthlessness that lock recipients into dependency; and the complex administrative structure prevents an investment in the time and skill required to offer constructive help.
>
> As a result, there has been a growing consensus that what is required is not more of the same, but new approaches. It has been demonstrated amply over the years, we think, that more investigations of eligibility are not the answer, that forced work is not the answer, that removing children from their homes is not the answer, that denying Federal assistance to intact families is not the answer, that welding services and income maintenance is not the answer.

The nation has 30 years of experience with these devices and the results are plain: they have not succeeded in controlling the caseload and they have not helped people. It is equally evident that some of the provisions in H.R. 12080—adhering as they do to the familiar route of control and threat—will fail. Aside from the morality of penalizing children with the proposed ceiling on the AFDC caseload, removing children from parents who decline to work and forcing mothers into work and training that may not be appropriate—there are also questions of practicality and effect.

It is our contention that these devices will not work to the end that H.R. 12080 envisions: a reduction in the number of Americans in need of public assistance. [We are] confident that the enactment in provisions for an AFDC ceiling, mandatory work and training and restrictions in the AFDC-UP program will increase the number of hearings and court challenges, aggravate tension in ghetto areas with a high proportion of welfare recipients, further cripple the administration of public assistance by multiplying areas of discretion, penalize the children who are already penalized by their families' reduced circumstances, and place intolerable financial burdens on states and localities that try to maintain their programs.

At a time when we are agreed that the problems of the urban communities pose the greatest challenge to our domestic policies, we are in danger, through this bill, of striking at the very group most involved. The admirable programs now under discussion in the areas of employment opportunities, better housing, improved police protection, revitalized education, and more accessible health programs could in large measure be vitiated by a return to more restrictive, coercive methods of public assistance.[8]

This testimony consciously uses social work values and knowledge, combines them in a way characteristic of social work, and effectively uses them to contribute to the welfare of a deprived

---

[8] "NASW Testifies in Senate on Social Security Bill," *Washington Memorandum,* September 8, 1967, p. 5.

and rejected group of people. Ginsberg and Thursz show a primary orientation to the welfare clients in emphasizing the stigma of welfare and the penalizing of the children. Feelings of worthlessness and dependency are produced, they say, by the methods of payment. The public assistance program, they further point out, has never succeeded in solving the problems it was designed to meet and the proposed AFDC provisions, based partly on threats and control, represent a backward step that will not work. The experience of social work that force is not effective with such complex problems and that programs cannot be imposed on people in this way is clearly presented.

In formulating social policy, social workers do not always bring out the particular social work contribution, which means presenting not only the social problems but also their meaning to the people involved. But in this example, the social work contribution is clearly and firmly presented. When put into operation in this way (see diagram, p. 130), the values become translated into *attitudes toward people* and the knowledge appears as a *way of knowing and understanding people and their needs.* Social workers have frequently been so concerned with service and action that they have not taken sufficient time to pause and examine the potential strength and force of this *value-knowledge component* that is at the very core of their profession. The attitudes are partly demonstrated by social workers' ways of working with people but are also translated into ideas that can be communicated to others. The understanding rests on and emerges from social work's approach to the growing knowledge derived from its own experience in working with people and from other sources.

It is interesting to consider what might have happened if social work had been ready earlier in the history of public assistance to use its full value-knowledge perspective and to look more directly at people and their problems. This required the ability to move beyond the restrictive compass of familiar concepts—such as agency, client, individualization, eligibility, and service—and to perceive large groups of people with common difficulties and deprivations. Social workers might then have become aware of how ineffectively these people were struggling to meet social problems that were beyond their capacity to solve—poverty, physical disability, old age, racial discrimination, poor housing, broken families, unemployment, and many others. This was a period when a change in social organization was taking place. Formerly, immigrants had been able to move out of the slums in successive waves because the expanding economy provided jobs. Soon the time would come when lack of such opportunity would produce immobilizing conditions of poverty and urban ghettos. Without understanding and help from society, the people caught in this situation would become isolated, helpless, and hopeless. If social work had developed its value-knowledge focus earlier, social work leaders might have been able to look beyond the public welfare program and alert society to this growing problem, which was later recognized and described in such a telling fashion by such writers as Harrington.[9]

In the NASW testimony before the Senate in 1967 (given by Ginsberg and Thursz), we see social work values and knowledge operating as a force to influence programs. Social workers have been much concerned with the power structure of the community. We should recognize that social work has its own power of a different kind, a power for constructive action for human better-ment, if it is fully acknowledged and put to work. The *attitudes* toward people and *understanding* of their needs, if recognized and used in combination, can have significant impact on social institutions. This is the priority of knowledge and value described in the Working Definition. Here is found the primary social work leverage for social change.

Social Workers' Ways of Viewing Social Situations

Social work values and knowledge, in the form of attitudes toward and understanding of people, are combined into *ways of viewing social situations* that are becoming increasingly character-istic of the profession. The diagram of assessment on page 149 showed some of the characteristics of social situations that are sig-nificant for social workers because of the common base of their profession. In viewing situations, values are translated into atti-tudes of respect for individual worth and concern for human

---

[9] *See,* for example, Michael Harrington, *The Other America: Poverty in the United States* (New York: Macmillan Co., 1963).

potential and growth.   Knowledge is translated into an understanding of the social tasks that people are facing, their ways of coping with them, the demands and supports of the environment, and particularly the consequences of the interaction for people. Knowledge and value continually interact in important ways. Attitudes toward people are strongly influenced by a dynamic psychology that provides awareness of irrational and unconscious aspects of behavior, emotional conflict, and ambivalence.   For a fuller understanding of social functioning, greater emphasis on rational aspects of behavior will be needed to balance the emphasis on emotional aspects.

Social workers' knowledge regarding social institutions is influenced by their concern for human potential and growth. As shown in the preceding example of the social workers' testimony before a Senate committee, in viewing social situations encompassing many people, such as population groups or large programs, the effort to understand the meaning of the situation to the people involved is an especially important characteristic of the profession. Social workers are concerned not only with developing more adequate resources but also with understanding why people so often seem blocked in using apparently available resources. Social workers consistently view social institutions in terms of their responsiveness to people's needs.   This social work way of viewing social situations is of major importance because it has its own essential characteristics that differ from and add to the perceptions of other helping professions and groups interested in social action.[10]

Interventive Approaches

As our examination of social work practice proceeds, the picture of the social work practitioner grows and changes.   In earlier practice he perceived himself as a "caseworker," "group worker," or "community organization worker" operating within a particular field.   Now we perceive him as starting from a defined professional

---

[10] *See* Harriett M. Bartlett, "Characteristics of Social Work," *Building Social Work Knowledge: Report of a Conference* (New York: National Association of Social Workers, 1964), pp. 1–15.

focus and orientation and a common base of value and knowledge, assessing the situations with which he is to deal, defining the social work contribution, and considering the profession's interventive repertoire, from which he identifies those approaches appropriate for the specific situation.

In recent years, as there has been growing recognition of the overemphasis on direct service to individuals and the need for social work to broaden its efforts in the direction of social policy, social planning, and social programs, one thinker after another has raised the question of whether there are two distinct paths or operations involved. Hamilton describes two practitioner models, one concerned with the treatment of clients and the other with programs, committee work, administration, and public relations.[11] Burns describes the "therapeutically and clinically oriented" and the "social welfare specialist" and maintains that they are so sharply distinct in their objectives and practice that they do not even have a generic base beyond a common philosophy, concern for people, and historical background.[12] Jane Hoey calls for the training of two groups, social practitioners and social strategists.[13]

Sometimes it is pointed out that persons who enter social work have interests and capacities leading them in one direction or another. At other times the distinction between the interventive actions themselves is stressed. One type of intervention, which involves direct service, is often described as "clinical," while the other is variously described as community practice, social welfare service, social planning, or some similar term. One group of social workers is assigned to one line of activity and another group to the other line, each with its own knowledge and interventive approach. It is agreed that both groups have common social work values but what else they have in common as members of the same profession is not clear, particularly in relation

---

[11] Gordon Hamilton, Editor's Page, *Social Work,* Vol. 4, No. 3 (July 1959), p. 2.

[12] Eveline M. Burns, "Tomorrow's Social Needs and Social Work Education," *Journal of Education for Social Work,* Vol. 2, No. 1 (Spring 1966), pp. 18–19.

[13] "One World—XIIIth ICSW," *National Conference on Social Welfare Bulletin,* Vol. 70, No. 1 (Fall 1966), p. 7.

to the knowledge base. An approach that looks to the future comes from Kendall, who distinguishes "people-helpers" from "system-changers." She indicates more clearly than did many earlier thinkers that both will have a common base of knowledge and values but suggests that there is a trend toward a "two-track" curriculum for the profession.[14]

Much of this thinking seems to be influenced by an educational approach, particularly as a reaction to the methods sequences and the long-continued predominance of casework in the curriculum. Since a curriculum has to be organized in the form of courses, there is a tendency to divide experience prematurely into logical categories. The practice orientation permits a more flexible approach to ongoing experience. Our examination of practice does not suggest such a two-track division between social work operations. It suggests instead that social work has an interventive repertoire comprising a considerable number of measures and techniques, which are used in various combinations by practitioners. Young practitioners start with competence in a few types of intervention and extend their competence to others as they gain experience. At one side of the profession are those who work primarily with individuals, families, and/or small groups. At the other side of the profession are those who work broadly with social conditions, programs, and social policy. In the middle is a large group whose members combine these approaches in a variety of ways. These social workers are consciously involved in both "people-helping" and "system-changing" and it is their awareness and competence in using the two approaches together that produce the effective results.

— One fact which stands out with clarity in our examination of practice is that the two major interventive approaches need each other. The direct service approach needs breadth. The community planning approach requires constant awareness of and sensitivity to the needs of individuals. Teaching a common body of values and knowledge in the classroom will not be enough. Through what has been known as casework, the profession has acquired the depth of understanding and quality of empathy with

---

[14] Katherine A. Kendall, "To Fathom the Future," *Journal of Education for Social Work,* Vol. 3, No. 1 (Spring 1967), pp. 21–28.

individuals that are essential characteristics. Through increasing participation in social planning, the profession is learning to broaden its contribution in response to the requirements of a changing society. In order to have both the necessary depth and breadth in its future practice, social work must ensure that both types of practice continue and what is learned through one is shared and used in the other. This means that students will need some meaningful experience in both areas of practice. It also means that the flow of experience in practice between those using the two approaches should be encouraged and kept open and no conceptual or educational barriers should be set up between them. The differences are less important than the fact that all practitioners should perceive themselves as social workers, working toward the same objectives with a common professional base.

Out of this discussion of intervention now emerges an important idea, namely, *the interdependence of the various approaches to helping people that have been developed and are now being used by social workers.* In this time of transition, when practice is in such a fluid state, it would be premature to move at once toward a two-track pattern in social work. History shows the social work tendency to make quick decisions about practice and education, decisions that have created barriers to the profession's further growth and tended to swing its practice too far in one direction or another. We can continue to recognize that social workers characteristically work through two channels—through a direct relationship with the people being served and through collaborative relationships with others—without regarding these channels as opposites. What is most important now is to examine the various combinations of interventive approaches that are being tried out in practice and to try to identify what it is that makes them peculiarly appropriate and effective for social work. This should be done at the practice level first before it is translated into curriculum.

New Perspectives on Intervention

How will the three traditional methods change as a result of movement toward the common base of social work, with its emphasis on the priority of value and knowledge and recognition of a wide range of interventive measures? This cannot yet be forecast accurately but a few implications can already be perceived. As has been pointed out, some of the knowledge formerly regarded as belonging to casework, group work, or community organization will now be recognized as essential for all social workers. Through teaching and practice, this knowledge, which has broader application, can be expected to move out from the confines of particular methods and become a part of the profession's basic body of knowledge. The concept of social functioning, if fully used, will require that all social workers be concerned with people interacting with their social environment. Thus the sharp differences among the traditional three methods are likely to be reduced, since all social workers will share a common perception of the situations with which they deal.

In a period of rapid social change it appears further that social work methods can no longer be practiced so separately and under such controlled conditions as in the past. All interventive measures are now used within a wider context because of the complex interrelationship of urgent social problems and the growth of comprehensive programs that combine multiple services. Thus the three methods must take their place along with other interventive approaches—whether old or new—in the full repertoire of the profession.

Social workers operating in the area of practice known as community organization approach problems of social functioning from the angle of social conditions and social institutions. In a project designed to outline educational preparation for community organization (under the auspices of the Council on Social Work Education), Arnold Gurin and his associates have developed some new thinking of significance for all social workers. They trace the long-standing emphasis on enabling people to enhance their social competence as an effort to fit community organization into the concept of process in line with the social work concept of method. They conclude, however, that this did not cover a good deal of what the social worker was doing and that in the present decade the emphasis has shifted substantially toward social change as a goal and social planning as a methodology. This means, they say, dealing with organizations and interorganizational systems with a view to modifying organizations and making them more effective in solving social problems.   They identify the three organizational types as *groups of people, service agencies,* and *interorganizational structures,* each with its own cluster of tasks. The practitioner's point of departure is from one of these organizational types and he works with them all.[15]   These are the moving parts of the social change process.   The practitioner must understand and exploit the connections between them but, in the opinion of Gurin and his associates, no general theory has as yet emerged from the social sciences or social work practice to meet this need.[16]

It will be of importance to the future growth of the profession how this approach to social change through "modifying organizations" is eventually related to and integrated with the social work focus on social functioning, the social work orientation to people, and other elements in the common base.

In view of the fragmentation of social work practice in the past through unco-ordinated agency programs and separate fields and the increasing difficulty of getting services to people, the question is being raised whether a practitioner who might be described as a "generalist," or general practitioner, is needed in social work. It should first be clear that one does not become a generalist simply by using two or more methods together.   If needed, such a professional role should rest on more fundamental criteria.   The most important conclusion to be drawn from this examination of practice would be that it is important first to establish the social worker who genuinely rests his practice on the common base of

---

[15] It would appear that the social worker in community organization, in his efforts to "modify organizations," will frequently be operating like earlier social workers who were attempting to influence social programs in the agencies in which they were working and like social workers today who are functioning in consultative positions in community programs.   It would be of value for the profession if these apparently similar activities could be analyzed and compared in such a way as to establish more clearly and solidly than has yet been possible the nature of *consultation* in social work and the directions in which it can be developed as a more effective interventive measure in social change.

[16] Robert Perlman and Arnold Gurin, "Perspectives on Community Organization Practice," *Social Work Practice, 1967* (New York: Columbia University Press, 1967), pp. 56–71.

178   THE COMMON BASE OF SOCIAL WORK PRACTICE

his profession. If all practitioners operate as *social workers,* with
the breadth of value, knowledge, and interventive competence
implied, problems of overspecialization and discontinuity of service
are likely to be greatly diminished.

Common Ways of Working with People

Out of the concept of the interdependence of interventive approaches emerges another idea. Just as there are general ways
of viewing social situations common to all social workers, so there
are *common ways of working with people* that can be distinguished
in social work practice. These are general characteristics of the
practice not tied to any particular methods.

Social workers characteristically share the assessment of the
situation and efforts to deal with it with those involved, whether
clients or others. At the same time, they emphasize the practitioner's self-awareness and the professional nature of the working
relationship. Thus on the one hand, they are participants in
the situation and on the other hand seeking a measure of separateness that will permit them to view the problems and alternatives
for action with professional objectivity.

Knowledge and values interact in influencing social workers'
ways of working with people. Particularly important is their
attitude of acceptance, which means perceiving and dealing with
the other person as he is, with all his strengths and weaknesses,
regardless of the nature of his behavior. It is distinguished from
approval and avoids overidentification.[17]

Social workers respect and emphasize the participation and initiative of people in dealing with their own problems as far as
possible. Kinds of participation that will strengthen people's coping efforts in known ways are encouraged. In selecting interventive approaches, social workers traditionally have preferred those
that stimulate growth and avoided those that involve domination
or manipulation of the people they are helping. Recognizing the
dynamic effect of attitude and understanding, social workers con-

---

[17] Felix P. Biestek, *The Casework Relationship* (Chicago: Loyola University Press, 1957), pp. 67–88.

sciously offer support to people overwhelmed by stress through their working relationship with them. In collaborating with others, such as planners, administrators, government officials, members of other professions, or citizen groups, to plan and render services, social workers regard this collaboration as a professional working relationship (as with clients), which involves respect for their manner of working and contribution as well as responsibility to further the joint effort.[18]

Such a description of common ways of working with people in social work practice endeavors to identify general patterns and thus to free thinking from the limitations of the method-and-skill concept. Such ideas as "one social work method" or "common elements in social work methods" have proved difficult to apply. They represent an advance toward a common base but cannot cover all practice. Common ways of working with people, used in association with the idea of common ways of viewing social situations, appear comprehensive and basic. Of course, a great deal of exploration and testing would be necessary to establish whether these are fruitful concepts for social work. However, they do seem to describe how social workers actually operate and to suggest important aspects of their distinctive contribution and thus seem to be useful directions of thinking for both practice and education.

Some Implications for Current Social Work Practice

Some further illustrations from current practice may help to clarify the ideas presented in the previous sections of this chapter. Because of the fluidity of social conditions today, there is more opportunity than usual for social workers to participate in the planning of new social programs. The initiative for the program may come from many directions—federal, state, and local governments, the social work profession, business or industry, or the people who are involved in the problems. The social worker may be participating as a member of his profession rather than as a representative of any specific agency. The program may be designed to meet either crisis needs or long-range problems.

The planning for new community programs is carried on by

---

[18] Bartlett, *op. cit.*

persons from many different fields and occupations who have their own interests and convictions, so that the social work viewpoint must be as clear and forceful as possible. It is especially important that it should not be presented from a single segment of practice or a single method approach but should represent the profession's fullest and strongest contribution. The social worker needs to be able to speak from the common base of social work. All that has been said about the power of ideas and the value-knowledge approach is pertinent here. In spite of well-intentioned planning, many new governmental programs do not take sufficiently into account the needs and interests of the people they are designed to serve, their problems in coping, their wish to participate, their lack of resources, and the negative attitudes often prevalent in the community toward such deprived groups.[19]

These are the very matters with which social workers are concerned and if they can find a firm place in the early planning, much wasted effort, confusion, subsequent conflict, and suffering on the part of people can be prevented. Sanders confirms this when, in discussing professional roles in planned change, he points out that social workers help other planners by indicating the implications of the plan for the welfare aspects and the client group and especially by keeping human considerations prominently to the fore. Others are aware of these goals, he says, but since these are not their primary concern, as they are for social workers, they too frequently get pushed aside in planning.[20]

In today's practice, programs to be assessed fall into such

---

[19] It is a further implication of this approach that the social work contribution should be identified before questions of strategy (in the sense of tactics and compromise) are considered. The realities of the situation will, of course, impose limitations so that the full contribution often cannot be made. If strategy is outlined first, however, the social work contribution never gets fully defined and thus some crucial elements may be lost. Until such time as the social work contribution is more generally recognized—by social workers themselves as well as others—and social work expertise in analyzing such complex situations is more fully established, it seems important to identify the profession's contribution clearly in each situation before strategy is considered.

[20] Irwin T. Sanders, "Professional Roles in Planned Change," in Robert Morris, ed., Centrally Planned Change: Prospects and Concepts (New York: National Association of Social Workers, 1964), pp. 104–110.

fields as family and child welfare, education, health, mental health (often separately organized), corrections, housing, and employment. New programs are continually being added. One useful contribution that social workers can make as part of their participation in program planning is to identify specific clusters of social tasks which are presented to the people and they must solve. These tasks are usually of two broad kinds: some grow out of the nature of the need or problem and others grow out of the program developed to meet the need, including its structure and organization, its scope and specific services. Thus in relation to health or mental health, individuals and families must deal with the tasks of illness and the problems of medical or psychiatric treatment and care. In a corrections program the individual must deal with the tasks associated with his status in society as a delinquent and with the special requirements of the correctional institution. The concept of social functioning assists the social worker in assessing the difficulties people have in coping with these tasks and what demands or supports the program, as well as other sections of their environment, is offering.

In some programs the major and only contribution of social workers may be their value-knowledge contribution early in the planning. If they have been successful in obtaining its inclusion, that may be enough because their attitudes and quality of understanding, infused into the service at an early point, can affect its whole quality and meaning for the people it is to serve and can thus influence all subsequent operations. It is probable that much of the hopelessness and anger of the people who suffer from poverty and the deprivation of civil rights results from the feeling that they are being demeaned and rejected by the rest of society. If social workers themselves steadily show an attitude of respect for and understanding of the people to be served by the program, this in itself can become a valuable initial influence in the planning process.

Another contribution which social workers can make relates to the recognition that it takes time to build up programs to the point at which they can actually reach the people, deliver services, and show results.[21] Many legislators and political leaders expect

---

[21] Melvin B. Mogulof, "A Developmental Approach to the Community Action Program Idea," *Social Work*, Vol. 12, No. 2 (April 1967), pp.

programs to start at once and apparently have no idea of the complexities and obstacles involved in getting services to people. Thus funds are too frequently voted for short periods and programs cut down or changed before they have begun to reach the people who need them. Furthermore, some programs, after being in operation for a while, are found to have unexpected gaps or unintended effects not beneficial to those involved.

In discussing "the perimeters of the possible" in institutional change, Brager recognizes a rather narrow margin of maneuverability for social workers and emphasizes education and persuasion.[22] Morris points out findings which indicate that "new ideas for change are seldom tolerated or well received unless the introducer is an intimate part of the organization to be changed or is at least accepted by it."[23] These findings suggest the opportunity that social workers may have to influence services when operating within large social programs.

In the thirties and forties social workers working in non-social work settings—such as medical care, mental health, and the schools—began to examine consultation and multidisciplinary teamwork as ways of influencing changes in these programs.[24]

12–20; and Peter Marris and Martin Rein, *Dilemmas of Social Reform: Poverty and Community Action in the United States* (New York: Atherton Press, 1967).

[22] George A. Brager, "Institutional Change: Perimeters of the Possible," *Social Work*, Vol. 12, No. 1 (January 1967), pp. 59–69.

[23] Robert Morris, "Social Planning," in Henry S. Maas, ed., *Five Fields of Social Service: Reviews of Research* (New York: National Association of Social Workers, 1966), p. 207. Morris refers to a study by Milton Lebowitz, "The Process of Planned Community Change: A Comparative Analysis of Five Community Welfare Council Change Projects," an unpublished doctoral dissertation, Columbia University, 1961.

[24] *See,* for example, Agnes Van Driel, "Consultation in Relation to the Administration of Social Service Programs," *Consultation* (Chicago: American Association of Medical Social Workers, 1942), pp. 5–10; Alice Taylor Davis, "Consultation: A Function in Public Welfare Administration," *Social Casework*, Vol. 37, No. 3 (March 1956), pp. 113–119; Florence Stein, "Teamwork in the Medical Setting: A Skilled Process," in Dora Goldstine, ed., *Readings in the Theory and Practice of Medical Social Work* (Chicago: University of Chicago Press, 1954), pp. 286–298; Doris Siegel, "Consultation: Some Guiding Principles for Medical Social Workers," in Eleanor Cockerill, ed., *Social Work Practice in the Field of Tuberculosis* (Pittsburgh: School of Social Work, University of Pittsburgh,

Practitioners who at that time experienced such consultation and teamwork at its best became aware of its possibilities as a way of improving the quality and scope of service to people. Such disciplined analysis and assessment of problems not infrequently represent a high level of collaborative thinking and action.[25] Social work's growing body of knowledge now widens the range and strengthens the impact of what social workers can offer through consultation and teamwork. In addition, the extension of their consultative activities and participation in program planning makes both these methods timely and important today. This may be one of the important directions in which social work practice will develop its potential for the future.

Innovative Changes in Practice

After the awakening in American society to the problems of poverty and civil rights and the recognition of the complex configuration of health, education, and welfare problems related to them, one of the first gaps in the social system was recognized as the failure to get services to the people who need them. Of special importance were efforts to restructure and reorganize the service system. Many social workers participated in these programs; in fact, there was such widespread concern throughout the profession regarding problems of service delivery that it was made the subject of a professional symposium sponsored by the National Association of Social Workers in 1968 under the title "Human Services and Professional Responsibility." [26]

In response to these needs, some voluntary agencies extended their services into the community in significant ways. One such undertaking by a family agency was the Youth Service Project discussed in an earlier chapter.[27] In another instance, an extensive project was undertaken by several national voluntary agencies, in fifty-nine communities throughout the country, to enable

---

1954), pp. 181–198; and Lydia Rapoport, ed., *Consultation in Social Work Practice* (New York: National Association of Social Workers, 1963).

[25] Harriett M. Bartlett, *Social Work Practice in the Health Field* (New York: National Association of Social Workers, 1961), pp. 71–74, 235–252.

[26] Willard C. Richan, ed., *Human Services and Social Work Responsibility* (New York: National Association of Social Workers, 1969).

[27] *See* pp. 157–159.

parents to improve their child-rearing practices through wider use of community resources.[28]

A further promising development is to be found in the initiative taken by professional social workers to establish agencies and programs themselves. Such leadership has been taken by a number of schools of social work to provide teaching centers for their students.[29] Another example is a special correctional unit developed under social work leadership.[30] The advantage of such programs established under social work auspices is that social work is freed from many of the restraints that so frequently develop under traditional agency auspices. The social work orientation toward people and their changing needs can prevail and the value and knowledge concepts and interventive approaches can be applied, demonstrated, developed, and tested.

New forms of service offer additional opportunities for social work practice. Combining the giving of service with collaborative action toward program-building is of particular significance in relation to multiservice centers. The idea of the multiservice center is spreading rapidly and being incorporated in federal and state legislation, thus becoming an important type of service organization. The major purpose is to make services more adequate and more available to the people who need them. Thus centers are placed geographically close to people. There is also emphasis on their being responsive to people's actual needs as they feel them, in contrast with the attitude of some professional workers and agencies who want to fit the person into their mold. For these reasons, it appears that multiservice centers are likely to remain more flexible in structure and procedures than traditional institutions. They do, however, frequently require the bringing together of a large number of services and types of personnel and can thus become complex. Social workers will be only one of many professional and nonprofessional groups of workers in these

[28] "Project Enable," *Social Casework,* Vol. 48, No. 10 (December 1967), whole issue. This issue is composed of five articles based on a project sponsored jointly by the Child Study Association of America, the Family Service Association of America, and the National Urban League.

[29] "Coordinated Services," *Children,* Vol. 14, No. 3 (May–June 1967), p. 125.

[30] Elliot Studt, Sheldon L. Messinger, and Thomas P. Wilson, *C-Unit: Search for Community in Prison* (New York: Russell Sage Foundation, 1968).

settings. Current experience suggests that bringing service personnel with varying orientations and expertise under one roof does not automatically solve the problem of discontinuity of services or produce good teamwork. More knowledge and experimentation plus much hard work will be needed to accomplish this.

As has been found in the past, collaborative work challenges each profession to identify its own contribution. This is to be seen particularly in the mental health centers that are spreading over the country under the Comprehensive Mental Health Act of 1963.[31] The field is wide open for creative exploration. The provision that these centers should include the functions of education and consultation has stimulated movement into the community. Social workers who formerly regarded themselves as clinical practitioners, trained as psychiatric social workers, are functioning as planners, administrators, educators, and consultants. They are combining these functions in a manner to demonstrate the combination of direct service and collaborative effort and the interweaving of varied social work interventive actions that have been described as being in the center of social work practice. Because the preventive approach to mental health naturally includes concern for people's adjustment to their life problems, the blurring of professional lines among psychiatry, psychology, social work, and other professions is one feature of the new practice.[32] This is an exciting experience for the participants and probably is helpful to families and communities in eliminating some of the old fragmentation of service. Social work is, however, the profession possessing what may prove to be the most difficult area of practice to define. In the flux of interprofessional practice, the "social" functions could be so spread among the various professional groups that the essential service would be diluted. The important issue here is not the defense of vested interests but that a growing profession which has a timely contribution to make

---

[31] *Planning of Facilities for Mental Health Services,* report of the Surgeon General's Ad Hoc Committee on Planning for Mental Health Facilities (Washington, D.C.: Department of Health, Education & Welfare, 1961).

[32] "Community Mental Health Centers: A New Social Institution in the Making," *NASW News,* Vol. 12, No. 3 (May 1967), pp. 16–20; and Bertram J. Black, "Comprehensive Community Mental Health Centers: Setting Social Policy," *Social Work,* Vol. 12, No. 1 (January 1967), pp. 51–58.

to society should continue on a course so that this contribution will be strengthened and not lost.

New Issues and Questions

Under the pressure of social change, the interest in social reform that characterized early social work and took the form of social action in later years returned with redoubled vigor. In the belief that the current system of social services was totally inadequate, some social workers pressed for efforts to change it radically at once. This activist approach frequently involved working with neighborhood and other interest groups with similar goals of change.[33] The groups brought pressure on city departments, welfare agencies, landlords, and others to make needed services available. Many voices were heard urging that social work should speak out and give leadership on vital national issues, such as the necessity for basic programs of income maintenance and social services for the whole population. Since social work could not and should not assume responsibility alone for such enormous problems, social workers interested in such action urged that it should be taken through coalitions strong enough to have impact on national social policy.

New ways of perceiving and defining social work roles and interventive approaches developed in the search for more effective measures. While social workers often assumed similar roles in the past, within the new context they appeared to have greater breadth and force. Because people need help in simply finding community services within the complex organization of our cities, social workers explored the role of guide, or *broker*, by offering intensive information about services. When this proved inadequate, a more aggressive role of *advocate* was defined. The social worker became a partisan in the conflict and a forceful defender of the client group's point of view. Working now in a political environment, many social workers became increasingly concerned with strategy, negotiation, and the use of conflict.[34]

---

[33] Robert Perlman and David Jones, *Neighborhood Service Centers* (Washington, D.C.: U.S. Department of Health, Education & Welfare, 1967).

[34] Charles F. Grosser, "Community Development Programs Serving the Urban Poor," *Social Work*, Vol. 10, No. 3 (July 1965), pp. 17–19.

Writing about changes in community organization, Grosser describes these trends in practice:

> In the past five years, largely under the influence of the comprehensive federal projects, community organization practice has moved from a method confined largely to chest and council social planning and the staffing of national social welfare agencies into extensive grass roots organization and participation in political areas. To its traditional concern with the orderly dispensation of existing welfare services, community organization practice has added an emphasis on social change, on serving groups in the community by altering institutional and other aspects of their environment. Once a method utilizing largely amelioration and consensus, it has grown to include the deliberate use of conflict and power. Community organization has added initiating to enabling. It has added working with the impoverished poor to working with the elite; it has added social agency criticism to social agency support.[35]

When social workers sought innovative actions in a variety of directions, however, it was not clear where some of these would lead. In some multiservice centers, delivery of service was combined with efforts to mobilize local residents toward community action. Thus situations arose in which community agencies, both public and voluntary, were being asked to co-operate in better delivery of service to individuals and families in the neighborhood at the same time that they were being subjected to aggressive pressure by community action groups organized to press for better service.

Seeking co-operation from community agencies while at the same time bringing pressure on them by neighborhood action groups leads to conflict and confusion. Rein and Reissman point out that this is not just a problem of administration but goes back to stance. In analyzing the antipoverty Community Action Programs, they argue that these programs can make their greatest contribution by adopting a "third-party stance." The best policy,

---

[35] Charles F. Grosser, "The Legacy of the Federal Comprehensive Projects for Community Organization," *Social Work Education Reporter*, Vol. 15, No. 4 (December 1967), p. 63.

they suggest, will be a combination of modified consumer advocacy with an effort to assist the traditional agencies.[36] Their
discussion refers to agencies but is also applicable to social work
practice, since social workers are employed in these programs.
The question then arises whether a permanently neutral position
between people and agencies would ever be appropriate for social
workers. Is not their primary identification with the people an
essential characteristic?

Further questions regarding social workers' stance and orientation arise in relation to the use of social action and advocacy in
pressing for social programs, whether community-wide or nationwide. What do action and advocacy rest on? They seem to
rest mainly on deep commitment to meeting the needs of the
poor and deprived, strategy in developing social policy and social
action, and pressure of numbers.[37] Many other liberal and radical
groups in our society operate in the same way. This kind of
action by social workers, in association with other groups, is important and likely to be effective for some time. But the time will
come when the existing institutions, the public, the legislators,
and the people themselves will ask social workers: On what authority does your action rest? What is your expertise, your special
knowledge, your particular contribution as a profession? What
more have you to give us for more effective and enduring solutions
to our social difficulties?

As social workers explore advocacy and activism, issues regarding social work's basic orientation must be faced. Some social
workers would consider that advocacy is most helpful if it is not
pushed to extremes, so that working relationships with resistant
agencies are maintained and programs can still be influenced
through collaborative efforts. If pressed to change beyond their
own pace, social institutions break down. Some social workers
would hold that in the instance of obviously inadequate programs
this may be the only answer. The question as to whether the
people who need the services will gain or lose in the end from

[36] Martin Rein and Frank Riessman, "A Strategy for Antipoverty Community Action Programs," Social Work, Vol. 11, No. 2 (April 1966), pp.
3–12.

[37] The Ad Hoc Committee on Advocacy, "The Social Worker As Advocate: Champion of Social Victims," Social Work, Vol. 14, No. 2 (April
1969), pp. 16–22.

the various types of advocacy is difficult to answer and requires constant exercise of sensitive and responsible professional judgment.

A further question to be considered is whether, in the search for innovation, social workers could overstress the role of conflict in politics. In their examination of city politics, Banfield and Wilson point out the trend toward the middle-class ideal, which emphasizes interest in the community "as a whole" and requires that authority be exercised by those who are "best qualified," that is, technical experts and statesmen, not "politicians." [38] Lane suggests that in what he calls our "knowledgeable society," knowledge is encroaching on politics. Under these conditions, he says, decisions are determined by calculations of how to implement agreed-upon values with rationality and efficiency, rather than by criteria for immediate political advantage. New knowledge sets up a disequilibrium that calls for action, as in the question of whether poverty, once recognized, is really necessary. He quotes Michael Harrington in pointing out that the people involved in the problem are often fatalistic but the scientist or professional views the causes and values more broadly and thus can point toward more socially constructive action.[39] Granted that forcible and even violent modes of problem-solving are increasing, social workers will need to be aware of this long-term trend toward greater use of knowledge in the rational solution of community problems and to ask themselves how they wish to make their contribution.

It would seem that a wide range of situations needs to be examined and evaluated in order to determine how social work knowledge, values, and interventive competence can best be used when there is conflict between people and service agencies or between people and the government.

Interventive Action in Relation to the Common Base

In discussing the "Working Definition of Social Work Practice" earlier in this monograph, it was suggested that the definition

---

[38] Edward C. Banfield and James Q. Wilson, *City Politics* (Cambridge, Mass.: Harvard University Press, 1965), p. 330.

[39] Robert E. Lane, "The Decline of Politics and Ideology in a Knowledgeable Society," *American Sociological Review*, Vol. 31, No. 5 (October 1966), pp. 649–662.

needed more flesh on its bones, that is, the content of the ideas needed to be filled in. The various components of the common base, as here developed, represent a beginning toward this content.

Now that more of the content is visible, we can better comprehend what is meant by the priority of knowledge and value. It can be seen that knowledge and value, used with the social work focus and orientation, are the solid substance on which interventive action rests. Once the full range of interventive measures is perceived and their independence recognized, the selection must be made between alternative measures when considering action in specific situations. Such selection is made through use of professional judgment in assessment, as previously described. Assessment rests on knowledge and values and decisions regarding interventive action rest on assessment. Thus the first four components of the common base—focus, orientation, knowledge, and value—all underlie intervention. In this sense, they have priority over techniques, methods, and any other forms of action in social work practice. This progression from ways of perceiving the situation that rest on social work knowledge and value through assessment to decisions regarding interventive action was shown and discussed in the practice example (the social worker in the hospital ward) presented at the beginning of this chapter.

Knowledge and value are the priorities, not only in the assessment of specific situations but also in the long-range growth of a profession and its practice. New knowledge and insights regarding values do, of course, continually emerge from ongoing practice and interventive action. During the early stages of social work's development, concern with intervention in the form of method and skill was dominant. Today we recognize that new knowledge emerging in practice should be lifted out of the various segments of practice and made available to all social workers through the building of a visible body of professional knowledge. Now that the profession is maturing, the growth of knowledge and a more comprehensive type of assessment permit a clearer view of all the essential components in practice and a better understanding of the manner in which they are combined and applied through interventive action.

11

building a
strong foundation

This exploration has been guided by the underlying idea that it is social workers' own perceptions of their profession and its practice that will mainly influence and determine their performance, that is, the nature of their practice. Thus the effort was to examine social work *thinking* rather than social work *action*. This approach, which is not the usual one, has proved useful to us in producing new ideas and insights.

Our emphasis has been upon the identity, initiative, and specific contribution of social work as a profession, as distinguished from the agencies in which its members are employed. Agencies and programs come and go, but professions, if they are relevant to society's needs, may persist for centuries. Agencies and programs necessarily focus on specific social problems and tend toward rigidity because of their bureaucratic organization. Professions, on the other hand, because they rest on broad goals and principles, are potentially more flexible and thus more responsive to social need.

Because social workers operate mainly as institutional employees, they have been faced over the years with the problem of developing their professional practice through their relationship with an enormously complex and rapidly changing system of

191

social institutions. As we know from our analysis, this effort has been only partially successful.

In this monograph, social work is viewed as a profession that primarily rests on and will grow through its values regarding man's potential and an increasingly scientific body of knowledge about social functioning, seen as the exchange between people and their social environment. Through these values and this knowledge, social work's interventive approaches and techniques will be developed and modified in response to social change. This value-knowledge-intervention complex becomes a heritage that is passed on by the profession to its members, providing them with a growing sense of identity and continuity. Since social workers belong to a service profession, the majority of whose members work directly with the people they serve, they can use their own experience to define people's needs and make use of but not depend entirely on the societal definition at any time.

In taking a broad look at practice, we must begin with the foundations. In this monograph the emphasis has been on bringing together significant ideas about the common base of social work practice, which has been retarded in its growth by the persistent fragmentation of practice in the past. Although of crucial importance, the common base cannot, of course, encompass all aspects of practice. In this chapter some steps needed to round out the analysis and development of practice in the social work profession, at its present stage of development, will be considered.

There are a number of subjects logically related to social work practice which require such extended discussion that they are beyond the scope of this monograph. Included in the original Working Definition was the concept of *sanction,* which covers the auspices under which practice is carried on, such as the society, the agency, and the profession itself. As indicated on page 59, because sanction does not operate within social work practice but is an outside influence, it has been discussed only indirectly here. The *educational implications* of a common base for social work practice are far reaching and of enormous significance for the profession. Movement toward such a base is also taking place in an increasing number of schools of social work. These developments in education and practice will influence each other and should progress together. The role of *research* in the development of the common base is also of major importance. Again this is a large subject in itself, which must be discussed by researchers who are thoroughly familiar with social work as a profession and the nature of its practice. Social work research has a unique and greatly needed contribution to make to the development of concepts and testing of generalizations related to the common base. The lack of any strong concentration of interest and effort in this direction in the past was one of the factors that delayed the development of such a base in the profession, particularly the building of a common body of knowledge.

In practice itself, whenever new directions of thinking emerge, much effort will be needed to examine and apply the ideas in discussion groups, professional committees, and other special projects of various kinds. Practitioners will have their own responsibility to clarify, extend, test out, and apply in practice the more comprehensive concepts now taking form.

There is another important feature, which has been mentioned from time to time, namely, that in the practice of all professions there are not only commonalities but also significant variations that must be recognized and understood. In social work variations in practice have been so important that they have tended to dominate social workers' approaches to their practice over a prolonged period. The problems involved in including them in an integrated professional practice have not yet been solved, but progress in defining the common base permits a new approach. It is suggested that there are three steps that urgently need to be taken, all of which are concerned with variations in practice as related to the profession's common base. They are as follows: (1) clarifying practice in specific problem and program areas as related to specialization, (2) rounding out knowledge for practice, and (3) defining professional competence. These steps are important because they will affect the impact of social work practice on social needs and social change in important ways. Each of these projects has its own particular implications and ramifications.

Specific and Specialized Practice

Questions relating to the nature of specialization have remained a persistent problem in social work education and practice. In

1951 Hollis and Taylor, in their study of social work education, pointed out that the chief reason for the inability to develop a satisfactory social work curriculum was "the lack of adequate criteria for determining what is *basic* and what is *specialized* in social work" and recommended that the nature of specialization in this profession should be studied and clarified.[1]   This step, however, has been continually put aside and has met with only partial solutions.[2]

Professional specialization usually means the breaking down of some larger entity into parts for better implementation because the whole has become too large and complex for individual practitioners to encompass.   Our analysis of early social work practice revealed a different pattern.   What was called "specialization" in the early history of social work was most often a preliminary stage of professional growth, what we described earlier as "a profession growing through its parts."

This characteristic of social work practice led to premature concepts of specialization.   There was experimentation in education and practice, which considered both fields of practice and methods as areas of specialization, but neither succeeded because the concept of specialization is only valid when there is a concept of a whole that can be divided into parts, as Hollis and Taylor pointed out.   The generic curriculum, developed in schools of social work in the fifties, did not prove definitive enough to establish a base because it was still fragmented by the three methods.   The needed clarification finally came from directing attention to practice itself.   The idea that the common elements are present in all social work practice and that variations result mainly from differences in emphasis and use—as stated in the "Working Definition of Social Work Practice"—proved to be more fruitful as a starting point for defining specialization.

As was shown in the discussion of professional judgment in as-

---

[1] Ernest V. Hollis and Alice L. Taylor, *Social Work Education in the United States* (New York: Columbia University Press, 1951), pp. 250 and 398.

[2] *See* Harriett M. Bartlett, "The Generic-Specific Concept in Social Work Education and Practice," in Alfred J. Kahn, ed., *Issues in American Social Work* (New York: Columbia University Press, 1959), pp. 159–190.   *See also* Herman Piven, "The Fragmentation of Social Work," *Social Casework,* Vol. 50, No. 2 (February 1969), pp. 88–94.

sessment, the social worker in practice deals with specific situations. The knowledge and interventive competence learned in a "generic" curriculum will be sufficient to enable him to deal with many situations. However, no social worker can practice long in a particular area of practice before he begins to need additional knowledge about the phenomena and characteristics, whether they concern school, neighborhood, urban decay, or other problems. Practitioners not long in practice cannot be regarded as specialists because specialization rests on extended study and experience from which true expertise develops. It becomes important, therefore, to distinguish this initial "specific practice" from the truly specialized practice of the advanced practitioner.

Confusion has arisen from the fact that social work covers a wide variety of social phenomena that appear to be different from each other and thus "special." However, as soon as a comprehensive, integrative concept like social functioning is used, the apparently different phenomena can all be recognized as manifestations of this one concept, which represents the profession's central focus. Thus from the beginning, young practitioners must be able to recognize all such phenomena as instances of social functioning. Social workers who concentrate over a prolonged period of study and practice on one manifestation of social functioning—e.g., in relation to health, education, or welfare—will acquire a depth and scope of knowledge in that area, capacity for situational assessment, and competence in selecting and applying appropriate interventive measures that will make them true specialists.

In the past, the terms "specific" and "specialized" have been used interchangeably in social work education and practice but it seems important to use them with greater discrimination. If the profession is to gain intelligent control over its own practice operations and develop the appropriate educational preparation, these two types of practice—the specific and the specialized—need to be examined and distinguished. The idea of a common base, the elements of which are applied together in practice but with variations according to the particular characteristics of the practice, brings together the concepts of generic and specific, of basic and specialized. It now becomes possible, and urgent, to move ahead in eliminating the confusions that have persisted over so long a period.[3] The premature "specialization" of the early days was not a valid notion. Social work needs the true specialist in practice, who will arrive at expertise through extended experience and study and who can contribute to the ongoing definition and clarification of professional practice, particularly the building of social work knowledge. When specialization has eventually been given its proper place in relation to the common base, then contributions from specialists will continually enrich the common base and fragmentation between the various parts and segments of practice will diminish, if not wholly disappear.

Rounding Out Knowledge for Practice

What is meant by building a body of knowledge for social work is not the aggregation of all the various types of information and knowledge that social workers happen to be using at any one time, but primarily the bringing together of concepts, generalizations,

---

[3] Development of competence to deal with such problems in practice requires more in the way of knowledge and interventive competence than can be provided in the master's degree program in schools of social work, particularly if a firm grasp of the common base is to be acquired. It is important, however, for every student, as a future social work practitioner, to learn the essential concepts and processes involved in applying the common elements to a particular area of practice, beginning with the concept of social functioning, and selecting and applying relevant social work knowledge (about problems and intervention) to the particular situation. Although this monograph does not attempt to deal with the educational implications of the analysis of practice, it can be pointed out that such learning cannot be obtained from the customary fieldwork experience in one agency but would require the student to make a comprehensive analysis of one practice area through such learning experiences as reading the sources, observation of and some participation in practice, seminar discussion, and final integration of the content in written form. Thus every student would go through the important learning experience of applying the common base in one area of practice and be prepared to repeat the process as a social worker in his own practice, in whatever field, area, or program he later practiced. See Arnold Gurin, "The Community Organization Curriculum Development Project: A Preliminary Report," *Social Service Review*, Vol. 42, No. 4 (December 1968), p. 432; and Bartlett, *op. cit.*, pp. 186–188.

theoretical statements, and other propositions particularly relevant for the profession's central focus and potential contribution to society. In the previous discussion it was shown how earlier knowledge consisted mainly of "pieces" of theory from various sources and practice principles from the profession's own experience, not held together by any effective integrative concepts. Thus the profession's knowledge lacked a visible form and structure. When clearer conceptual organization is achieved, social workers will not have to move so unevenly by trial and error to identify the knowledge needed in their practice. They can increasingly use the key concepts of social work to guide them in their selection of knowledge propositions and in the process of relating them to practice. Since emphasis will be placed on concepts and themes, social workers will also have to be able to seek, find, and apply in their practice the specific knowledge that supports these propositions.

In the chapter on social functioning the usefulness of such a comprehensive integrative concept in bringing together the various segments of the profession's knowledge was discussed. That discussion emphasized the common base. For rounding out the complete body of knowledge, attention must also be given to the specific aspects of practice, as described in the preceding section. Considerable exploration and experimentation will be needed to see how to develop common and specific knowledge more effectively within the profession's overall body of knowledge. A few aspects will be discussed now to suggest the nature of the problem.

Presumably, the profession's common body of knowledge will cover propositions relating to the range of social phenomena and social situations with which social workers are concerned, as well as the range of interventive measures within the profession's repertoire. Such knowledge is important and relevant for all social workers. The knowledge needed for specific or specialized practice may appear mainly as a deepening and extension of this common knowledge in particular directions, as indicated and needed for practice in particular areas. It will be recalled that in practice the common elements are applied with variations. Additional knowledge peculiar to particular practice areas will also be included, such as the technical aspects of adoption in child welfare.

As was pointed out earlier, some of the basic knowledge—in relation to individual or group behavior, response to stress, or ways of seeking help—is embedded in the methods and should be made available to all social workers. The process of extracting such knowledge, which has already been organized in a particular form, may prove more difficult than starting with new knowledge. In reporting on possible future curriculum content for community organization practice, Gurin points out that much of this content is appropriate for all social work students and certain sections useful for students concentrating on various segments of practice.[4] If new knowledge can be assessed as common or specific when it is introduced into practice or the curriculum, the profession will be spared many of the confusions it faced in the past.

The problem of assessing and integrating new knowledge is illustrated by a recent development in practice. Mounting social pressures in society are leading some social workers to move toward the social problem area as the most timely and relevant area of concentration for the profession. This approach has the advantage of focusing on social phenomena and thus avoiding the limitations of the methods framework. The concept is not, however, easy to define. Who decides what is a social problem—society or the people involved? If both decide, what is the interaction between their perceptions?[5] The profession's orientation to people would influence social workers to give priority to the implications for the people involved. Maas and Turner, who propose the social problem approach, show the social work orientation by using the term "human problems." Maas stresses social work's humanistic ends and Turner emphasizes its concern with human development.[6]

Such knowledge is certainly relevant for social workers but difficulties arise if it is to be regarded as a major area for specialization. When social problems are presented and discussed—

4 *Ibid.,* p. 433.

5 *See* Arnold M. Rose, "Social Problem," in Julius Gould and William L. Kolb, eds., *A Dictionary of the Social Sciences* (New York: Free Press, 1965), pp. 662–663; Nathan E. Cohen, ed., *Social Work and Social Problems* (New York: National Association of Social Workers, 1964); and Irving Weissman, *Social Welfare Policy and Services in Social Work Education* (New York: Council on Social Work Education, 1959), pp. 44–55.

6 Henry S. Maas, "Social Work Knowledge and Social Responsibility," *Journal of Education for Social Work,* Vol. 4, No. 1 (Spring 1968), pp. 37–48; and John B. Turner, "In Response to Change: Social Work at the Crossroad," *Social Work,* Vol. 13, No. 3 (July 1968), pp. 7–15.

whether in social work or social science—all too frequently they are listed as discrete social phenomena. Unless the concept of human problems is fully related to the social work focus, its use in developing a new type of practice specialization could become another way of fragmenting social work practice. Comprehensive integrative concepts, such as social functioning, would need to be rapidly developed and applied to prevent such a result.[7]

Occasionally one finds a multidisciplinary presentation of theory which includes social work and is so presented that it is immediately relevant for social work practice. One example is a report of the work done at the Harvard School of Public Health, over a period of several decades, on the healthy child, his physical, psychological, and social development.[8] The principles of growth and development set forth are basic for all social workers in their understanding of the individual. In addition, throughout the volume, professional and scientific knowledge and theory from biological, psychological, and social sources are continually integrated. The section on the pregnant woman, the fetus, and preparation for maternal care, written by representatives of obstetrics, pediatrics, psychiatry, nutrition, and social work, is a good instance of such integration. Such a volume offers both general principles for all social workers and extended, specific knowledge appropriate for social workers concerned particularly with the needs of children.

Some social workers resist the idea of "social work knowledge"

---

[7] One way in which such integration could be approached is suggested in the discussion of assessment of social situations (pp. 143–153) in which "problems (conditions) of central concern" and "behavior and responses of people involved in the problem" are included as items characteristically viewed by social workers when they start from the common base of social work practice. In an earlier analysis of social work practice in the health field, the writer included two chapters on knowledge (concepts and theoretical propositions) from the health field and from social work, with discussion about how social workers related one to the other. In spite of their necessary limitations at the present stage of the profession's development, such analyses of specific knowledge related to basic knowledge are important for the development of practice. *See* Harriett M. Bartlett, *Social Work Practice in the Health Field* (New York: National Association of Social Workers, 1961), chaps. 7 and 8.

[8] Harold C. Stuart and Dana G. Prugh, eds., *The Healthy Child: His Physical, Psychological, and Social Development* (Cambridge, Mass.: Harvard University Press, 1960), Sec. 3, pp. 41–86.

as being too limiting, which would be true if it were confined to narrow segments and detailed aspects of practice. In such knowledge-building, it is of course important that the subconcepts should not be allowed to dominate the comprehensive integrating concepts. Interest in developing role theory or organization theory for social work use could become so absorbing (as it has in the past) that attention could be diverted from the development and application of overall concepts needed to make these specific approaches useful and relevant for social work practice.

In an educator's approach to social work knowledge, Hale suggests that knowledge-building be focused on the use of knowledge in practice. He points out the need to "define the structure of social work's knowledge base and factor out the principles, ideas, and generalizations that give shape to practice." [9] He further points out that a weakness of the present educational system has been to divert school faculties from one of their primary tasks— that of knowledge-building. The evidence of our analysis of the profession's growth confirms that if educators had been more active in building the profession's basic knowledge in relation to its practice before its incorporation into the school curricula, the fragmentation of practice and the problems of specialization probably would have been greatly diminished.

Professional Competence

Definition of professional competence is a third step urgently needed at this time, if the profession is to make its contribution to society.[10] Our analysis of early practice showed how the method-and-skill model limited the profession in its ability to arrive at an authoritative definition of its own competence. During the late fifties and early sixties, various committees of the National Association of Social Workers worked at the problem of defining competence from various angles. They were, however, blocked and confused by their need to think within the methods frame of ref-

---

[9] Mark P. Hale, "Focus and Scope of a School of Social Work," *Journal of Education for Social Work*, Vol. 3, No. 2 (Fall 1967), p. 47.

[10] Definition of competence was emphasized as a major undertaking for the future in the beginning of this monograph on p. 18.

erence, with which they were most familiar in viewing practice, particularly that of casework. Finally in 1964, the NASW Committee on the Study of Competence, under the chairmanship of Ruth I. Knee, took the necessary step of moving from the part to the whole of practice. The process is described in the committee report as follows:

> The Committee was aware of the implications of beginning the study of professional competence with the use of any particular method or field of practice. However, during each stage of work a conscious effort has been made to broaden the perspective so that Committee deliberations would be pertinent to all of social work practice. The Committee discovered that generalizations about any one aspect of competence, when sufficiently refined, would match readily with different modes of professional intervention. The components of competence seem to apply equally well to all of the methods as well as the many fields of practice. The "client" might be seen as a person, a couple, a family, a group, an agency, or a community. The worker's auspices and collaborative arrangements might vary without excessive damage to the schematic design erected.[11]

By 1968 the NASW Committee on the Study of Competence was able to publish a comprehensive statement, based on consultation with many practitioners from all areas of practice. The major components of competence in social work practice were identified as (1) professional knowledge and understanding, (2) professional qualities and attributes, (3) professional practice, and (4) work management and relationships. Here at last was a scheme for identifying the criteria for the competence of social work practitioners that rests on the common base of the profession. Starting from a brief definition of social work practice derived from the Working Definition, the report says: "This suggests that the core elements in practice that underlie competence include knowledge and understanding basic to the profession as a whole, internalized commitments to basic values and purposes, and prac-

[11] "Report of the Committee on the Study of Competence to the 1964 Delegate Assembly" (New York: National Association of Social Workers, 1964), p. 4. (Mimeographed.)

202   THE COMMON BASE OF SOCIAL WORK PRACTICE

tice behavior that integrates knowledge, skill, and values in actual performance." [12]   Variations in practice (particularly by method and field) are to be recognized in determining competence.

The concept of professional practice used by the committee applies to the technical practice behavior of the individual social worker. In this monograph it has been found necessary to adopt a more inclusive concept of social work practice, which encompasses the profession's practice as a whole, in order to identify clearly the essential elements on which the individual social worker's practice must be based.   Some social workers consider professional competence to be the performance of the individual worker as defined by professional standards and do not inquire further on what these standards rest.   The base obviously must be the profession's body of knowledge, values, and interventive measures, without which the professional standards and practitioner's competence would not long retain their validity.[13]   As attention is directed to implementing the assessment of competence through various methods of testing the practitioner's performance, it is also of great importance that effort should not be diverted from continuing to clarify the elements of professional practice that must be assessed.   Much work still needs to be done on concepts and criteria before what can and should be tested in the professional practice of social work can be known.[14]

---

[12] Committee on the Study of Competence, "Guidelines for the Assessment of Professional Competence in Social Work" (New York: National Association of Social Workers, 1968), p. 2. (Mimeographed.)

[13] It is of interest to note that social work as a profession seems to have developed its approach to competence in the opposite order from what is customary.   Professions usually develop essential components of knowledge, value, and technique, which are transmitted through education and incorporated by individual practitioners.   Social work, on the other hand, first concentrated on incorporation of skill by the practitioner, then developed its educational curriculum, and only recently has started to identify the essential elements that comprise its practice as a profession.

[14] In "Guidelines for the Assessment of Professional Competence in Social Work," the knowledge, skill, and attributes identified are those that characterize the "self-regulated" practitioner—one who has progressed beyond the level of the newly graduated practitioner holding a master's degree from a school of social work.   In accordance with objectives set by the 1960 NASW Delegate Assembly in establishing the Academy of Certified Social Workers and later action taken by the 1969 Delegate Assembly, qualitative requirements for admission to the Academy will become effec-

Further Steps in the Common Base: Relationship of Components

In building the model of the common base of social work practice, it was necessary to develop the components one after another—first knowledge, value, and interventive action; then the central focus on social functioning and the primary orientation to people. In looking to the future and continuing to build up the substance of the common base, a major consideration becomes the relationship between the various components, with recognition that they are and must continue to be related. The identification and description of the nature of this relationship is of major importance because, unless this is done, the common base itself will fall apart, just as practice was continually being divided in the past.

In this monograph a beginning was made by describing the priority of knowledge and values and the manner in which they are used together (but still kept distinct) in social work practice. Because all the other components depend on knowledge, the need for building a strong body of knowledge has been repeatedly stressed. Since knowledge must have a focus, the need for a clarified central focus for the profession and integrative concepts to support this focus has also been emphasized. At present, concepts and generalizations used in social work practice are so unrelated and scattered that they can hardly be recognized by persons either inside or outside social work as the common base of a single profession.

Thus the next important and greatly needed step would seem to be to identify a small number of concepts and generalizations that would be so related as to be integrative for the profession.[15] Some

---

tive in 1971. Plans are under way for the Council on Social Work Education to raise the standards of undergraduate programs of social work education. NASW will share responsibility with other organizations to identify the areas of practice and the competence of the practitioners admitted to the association through the action to broaden the membership in 1969. In the author's opinion, measures for testing competence and curricula for educating practitioners will only be valid insofar as they rest on continuing study and clarification of the essential components of social work practice.

[15] *See* the discussion on "Lack of Social Work Concepts," p. 46 of this monograph.

of these might have to do with coping behavior, the social environment, and what goes on in the exchange between people and their environment. Some might have to do with the concept of man as growing and developing throughout his life, with special concern for understanding human potential. Some might have to do with the development of social institutions that would be more responsive to man's long-range needs than they have been in the past. In other words, the concepts and generalizations for this knowledge-building would be developed in key areas. Professional responsibility would require the testing of the knowledge generalizations as rapidly and steadily as the profession's resources would permit.

Another aspect of the relationship between components in the common base, urgently calling for clarification, is the connection between knowledge and values on the one hand and interventive action on the other. Suppose the practitioner has mastered the core concepts and generalizations as they are later defined; then how does he apply them in his practice? It is here that the use of professional judgment in assessment of situations is crucial and that is why this monograph has stressed the importance of a broad type of social work assessment, not confined to methods but capable of encompassing and using all the components in the common base.

It will be remembered that the practitioner starts from the profession's base—otherwise his practice would not be social work—and then moves into the particular aspects of situations as indicated. His specific knowledge and practice always rest on the common base. As the key concepts and generalizations discussed previously are developed, it would become important to explore how they can best be used to guide practitioners in selecting and applying the knowledge needed in practice.

One further aspect of practice contributes particularly to the relationship of the components in the common base and helps to hold them together, namely, the common characteristics of social work practice that cut across the various components which emerged in the early days of practice. They are the common ways of viewing people and situations, the common ways of working with people (clients and others), and such recognized characteristics as the self-awareness and professional discipline of the individual practitioner.[16] These characteristics, although not always clearly verbalized, are pervasive and persistent throughout social work's practice and literature. As the components in the common base are developed in the direction of a more orderly system, it is important that these general characteristics, which in their particular way contribute to the essential nature of social work, should not be lost.

Thinking, Feeling, and Doing

Strengthening the knowledge component in the common base calls for practitioners who can use the new concepts and generalizations in combination with the profession's values and interventive measures. The major components in the individual social worker's practice have frequently been described as "thinking, feeling, and doing." Until recently, as has been pointed out, feeling and doing were emphasized. Not only was thinking not stressed, but sometimes intellectual operations were avoided as somehow alien to social work. This monograph has emphasized the need to strengthen the cognitive and intellectual aspects of practice. The use of knowledge and ideas is inherent in the nature of professions. Furthermore, the growing common base requires social workers who can master its content, particularly its concepts and knowledge.

The question might be asked why the development of the curriculum and fieldwork has claimed so much attention in social work education. Recognizing that no person can acquire in school all the knowledge and skill necessary for his practice, the major professions are increasingly giving priority to the need to produce graduates who can master and apply in practice the concepts and generalizations essential to their profession. Conant and Dubos both stress the intellectual equipment needed for thinking in terms of concepts and theory as being the best preparation for dealing with new situations in an ever changing world.[17] The idea of self-regulated practice and the autonomous social worker who will be less dependent on supervision and agency practice than in the

---

[16] See pp. 34, 36, 142, 171, and 178.
[17] See pp. 39–40 and 108–109.

past is now growing in social work.[18] Such a practitioner is able to use knowledge in the form of concepts and generalizations (not just as information) and to apply it consciously and rationally in his practice. Not everything a professional worker does can be so defined and systematized; the art of practice still remains important. However, feeling and doing (attitudes and interventive action) now become more effective because of the greater emphasis on thinking.

Social workers have often called for "social work statesmen" who can be leaders, but more than the capacity to think in terms of social policy is needed today. The social worker who masters relevant knowledge through broad concepts is likely to make the most creative contributions to social planning and professional practice. Young workers who leave school with a command of concepts that enable them to perceive the essentials of their profession also will progress further in their own practice than when thinking was subordinated to feeling and doing. Thus the "autonomous worker" is actually more closely related to his profession's base than ever; he is one who is competent to master, use, and perhaps himself contribute to its basic principles.

One aspect of conceptual thinking that is particularly relevant for social work has to do with the use of models in thinking about practice. Models are likely to be helpful to social workers at the present time for temporary use in clarifying relationships among various factors with which they must deal. Social workers have been aware of the many variables in social situations but less successful in finding ways of relating them to each other. In this monograph models have been used to view and analyze complex aspects of practice; they have proved helpful in revealing both the connections and the gaps in thinking.

As was shown in the earlier discussion of barriers to integrative thinking, some social workers are fearful that models are too controlling. Actually, perspectives and frames of reference are positive devices for more effective thinking. They give professions their distinctiveness; they identify what is characteristic and thus give the practitioner security; they describe what is common so

---

[18] "Guidelines for the Assessment of Professional Competence in Social Work," p. 4; and Hale, *op. cit.,* p. 40.

that thinking can converge; they are essential for effective communication, which requires that people be in the same universe of discourse; they are essential for cumulative thinking and theory-building. The profession needs to find a way to make all its members comfortable in using these intellectual approaches and in taking time to think.

The common base of social work practice, as suggested in this monograph, is the beginning of a frame of reference for social work. Such frames ordinarily grow from the contributions of many members from all parts of a profession. Social workers who are fearful of "global thinking" would probably have more confidence if they could see this process taking place gradually. However, the times are urgent and social work cannot afford to wait too long to marshal its strengths.

Testing Practice Innovations Against the Common Base

The problem of dealing effectively with practice innovations during times of crisis demonstrates well the need to define the relationship of the essential elements in the profession's practice. Professions must always keep growing, but if changes are numerous, scattered, and involve sharp breaks with current practice, there is danger that they cannot be absorbed. In addition, if the profession is in an active stage of building its common base, there is the further risk that this vital movement may be so slowed up or diverted that the whole growth of the profession will be seriously obstructed.

If new approaches to interventive action are borrowed from outside sources, such as business, law, or government, it is most important to make clear the similarities and differences between the way they are used in these other contexts and in social work. For example, the lawyer acting as an advocate pleads for his client and defends the confidentiality of their relationship. Some lawyers also plead for social justice for groups of people. In these aspects, law and social work are in full accord. There are important differences, however, in the nature of the help the lawyer gives his client. He does not allow himself to be drawn into a relationship directed toward helping the client or group deal with the consequences of their actions as affecting their future life. Furthermore, the ultimate decision regarding action is made by the judge, based largely on law and legal precedent, so that the lawyer has a distinctly different responsibility than the social worker in relation to the kind of professional assessment of the situation he makes and the scope of action he undertakes. Unless such distinctions are recognized and evaluated when concepts are borrowed from other professions, latent and unresolved confusion can develop and persist in social work practice. Furthermore, social workers should not forget the problems that resulted when the concept of "treatment" was borrowed from medicine without differentiating its use in a clinical context from its use by a profession that also serves groups and communities. Because of these problems of interpreting and integrating approaches from outside sources, social workers may in the long run find it clearer to adopt neutral terms (such as assessment) and give them precise social work meanings. Actually, social work is probably past the point in its development when it needs to borrow so frequently and continually from the outside.

Furthermore, practice innovations no longer need to be launched as isolated actions because innovators can now test them against the common base. In such instances, the innovator is evaluating the place of his suggested innovation within the practice of his profession, just as he might assess a more limited problem to determine his own interventive action. He asks himself: How does the approach relate to social work's body of values, knowledge, and interventive measures? How does it relate to our concept of social functioning and orientation to people?

The purpose of innovation is, of course, to extend social workers' services to more people and to strengthen social work's role in social change. Thus it becomes necessary to examine the proposed innovations to determine whether they fall within the focus and competence of social work and to distinguish them from actions that are more effectively and appropriately carried on by others (such as other professions or citizens' groups). No matter how urgent or attractive the new line of action may appear, the innovator must face directly the question of whether it is within social work's competence and a sound direction for its future development. In other words: Is it social work?

In their commitment to social justice and human rights, social workers feel themselves impelled toward action. But how long is this action likely to be effective in its impact on society unless it is based on a solid and growing body of professional knowledge? Furthermore, in moving beyond the one-to-one relationship with clients to work with families, neighborhood groups, or social programs, there is another danger, namely, that some social workers may transfer their basic values regarding individuals to these new approaches. It must never be forgotten that whatever the approach—whether through large populations or nationwide social institutions—the ultimate aim is the growth and self-ful-fillment of individuals, since this is the only way that man can attain his potential. Problems such as these, centering around the relationship of knowledge, value, and interventive action, are yet to be solved in social work.

If the innovators who move into action do not themselves ex-plore the relation of their actions to the common base, does it not become the responsibility of educators and researchers to do so? Some of the questions to be answered might be these: What are the theoretical roots of the new approach? On what knowl-edge generalizations and value concepts does it rest? Are these fully understood and in what ways have they been tested? What are the implications of these generalizations and values for social work and its capacity for service? Can they be absorbed into its common base in such a manner as to enlarge and strengthen its practice? What must social workers do in the way of examining values, defining concepts, and stating and testing generalizations to attain such a result? How would some of the current develop-ments in social work practice, such as advocacy, family treatment, or new trends in social action, appear when so examined? Social work's past experience shows that unless such developments are carefully assessed, they can persist as latent sources of difficulty and producers of negative, unintended by-products in ongoing practice.

Urgent Questions Facing the Profession

Since the relationship of the components in the common base is such an abstract idea, we must ask ourselves what this means in terms of practical steps to be taken and work to be done by the profession in the years just ahead. Here are some of the steps that are strongly indicated because they are of a kind that can lead to further steps and thus toward cumulative growth for social work:

▪ To make the *common base* of social work practice clear and meaningful to students in schools of social work and workers in practice. This means carrying on the work begun in the "Working Definition of Social Work Practice" to establish a strong foundation for all social workers to use together.

▪ To build social work's *body of knowledge,* not through gathering a mass of information but through developing a limited number of core concepts and generalizations focused on social work's area of central concern (social functioning). Just as the idea of coping leads to the idea of consequences for people's growth, so these central concepts should lead to each other and all be interrelated.

▪ To perceive and develop professional *competence* as resting primarily on the full and growing strength of the profession's bodies of knowledge and value. Competence viewed as the "doing" of the individual worker, developed largely through apprenticeship training, will not be adequate to deal with the complex problems of our changing society.

▪ To establish more clearly the primary *orientation* of social workers toward the people they serve. This is related to but differs from the client-worker relationship in direct service and agency stance in program planning. The broadening and often conflicting responsibilities of social workers in neighborhoods and social programs call for more penetrating analysis and definition of the profession's primary and consistent orientation toward people —and ultimately toward the individual—as related to but differing from its other orientations toward agencies, government, citizen groups, and the community.

▪ To identify the pattern of social work thinking in *assessment* of social situations so that it can be learned and consistently used by all social workers. This is a central professional process urgently calling for attention, since the effectiveness of social work interventive action depends on the validity of the assessment on which it is based.

■ To close the persistent gap between what is *"special"* and what is "common" or "basic" in social work practice, that is, to get the variations in practice firmly integrated with the common base. The principles by which the variations in social work practice—whether in the form of knowledge or interventive action —can be consistently related to the common base should be established and demonstrated, so that practice innovations and new developments will no longer become divisive elements and "foreign bodies" in the profession's practice, as they have been in the past.

■ To develop social work intervention, not in the form of separate "tracks" or "methods" but as interrelated types of *interventive action,* that is, the interventive repertoire of a single profession. This means exploring how competent practitioners use interventive measures in various combinations to further social work purposes, as in using direct service and consultation to supplement each other. Here the disciplined use of knowledge and value together is of particular importance.

Now that social work has a visible and growing common base, its members can no longer afford to undertake the kind of unintegrated thinking and action that, in the past, led to new kinds of fragmentation. If a profession is to endure and make an effective contribution to humanity, its knowledge must continue to grow with respect to its interventive action. When the goals of its practice become detached from the bases of its expertise or its aspirations for people (which it tries to implement) are not reasonably underpinned with useful knowledge and techniques, the profession is in trouble. The approach suggested in this monograph aims to give a sufficient focus for both practice and knowledge-building so that they can develop together.

The types of relationship among the components in the common base mentioned here are illustrative of the steps that urgently need to be taken next but do not by any means exhaust the possibilities. Many other places where links among knowledge, values, and interventive action require clarification and strengthening will be found. What is important is to develop the common base so that it has the solid substance and broad scope necessary to enable it to be used confidently and effectively by all social workers in meeting the enlarged responsibilities that lie before them.

Integrative Thinking and Action

How can social workers best put to work their knowledge, their values, and their interventive expertise toward opening opportunities for people to live and grow in today's society and in the world of the future?

If all members of the social work profession perceived themselves as *social workers* operating from the same base, using shared values and knowledge and the same range of interventive measures, the profession's impact on social change would be increased significantly. The likenesses are more important than the differences. Through current practice and education, practitioners have no idea of the force that would inhere in a comprehensive and integrative concept of their profession and its practice. In their practice, teaching, and writing, social workers have been influenced by ideas that divide—dichotomies and polarities—such as "cause and function" or "two career lines." Such ideas can be clarifying if used within a larger frame but, without such a frame, become divisive, as has occurred too often. This can be seen in the difference between the impact of limited ideas covering just one area of practice—like family welfare or community development—and a comprehensive concept like social functioning. When and if this concept is fully developed and made operational by the whole profession, social workers can help people with their coping and can work to change social conditions in many different ways within an overall pattern. But unless social workers operate together on a sufficient number of basic concepts, unless they work together to strengthen their profession rather than divide it, social work could split apart.

The question should be asked whether in their strong commitment to meet human needs and rights social workers have faced what this means in terms of their own responsibility. It certainly means speaking out regarding people's needs and taking action in their behalf. But as has been indicated, advocacy and action must rest on more than concern. A major responsibility of a profession is the progressive development of its knowledge and competence. It is in this area that social work has shown less persistence and accomplishment than in other areas of professional responsibility, such as developing professional schools and organizations. There has been more concern and progress with structure and action than with building substance.

In this connection, two important lessons are to be learned from the analysis of social work's development. First, it can be seen how small perceptions of practice can build up to a general model that comes to dominate the thinking of the profession and is not submitted to a rational analysis of whether the approach favors or, on the contrary, may actually restrict the potential for growth. This is an important lesson to learn because social change might again precipitate social work toward other types of models that might become equally limiting in other ways. The current pressure for social action, if not kept firmly related to basic knowledge and competence, could draw social work practice away from its base in the same unintended manner and with the same negative results that occurred in the past with other incomplete practice models. Second, when parts and pieces of practice, which have become divisive through their very separateness, are placed within a larger framework, that is, brought together in a common base, they can begin to operate in such a way as to contribute positively to the profession's practice and growth. What was formerly a tendency to fly apart can now be transformed into movement toward co-ordinated effort and eventual integration.

The importance of the order in which certain steps in thinking follow each other is to be noted. The profession must first have a central focus before it can develop its own body of knowledge and integrate knowledge from other sources. Definition of the essential social work contribution comes before outlining the strategy for applying it. Likewise, assessment comes before action.

The way we perceive our experience is crucial. Some of the most serious barriers and gaps in the profession's growth have developed because of an overemphasis on some aspects and lack of awareness of others that were equally important. In our analysis of practice, it was clear that the way in which the social worker perceived his work was of primary importance. If the perception was narrow, the practice was restricted in its execution, no matter how skillful the worker. If the practitioner perceived his work as resting on a broad professional base, began with an assessment of the situation based on social work values and knowledge, and was flexible in combining appropriate interventive actions, the work was broader and potentially more responsive to the demands of social change.

Looking to the Future

This discussion has assumed that social workers can make their greatest contribution to society through a strong profession and a clear common perspective. Thus all the problems they want so urgently to deal with in this period of social change, such as income maintenance, manpower problems, new forms of delivering service, and social action, will be met more effectively. For instance, the support that social workers give to the development of broad programs, provisions, and services for all citizens should be infused with social work's values and knowledge about people and their social functioning. Also, social workers can most effectively aid the many technical and nontechnical workers needed in social welfare today if they have something additional and distinctive to give, which is based on well-recognized competence. It is, therefore, tremendously important that the profession should be steadily working to develop its own strengths at the same time that it is meeting the current needs in society.

Social work as a profession urgently needs to make provisions by which continuity of thinking regarding social work concepts, generalizations, theory, and knowledge-building can be assured. The research centers established in several schools of social work are a step in the right direction but do not provide the kind of cumulative thinking that is essential. A permanent advanced center associated with a university is needed. Such a center should be protected from pressure in order to promote the kind of long-range thinking and stimulation of communication among thinkers that is required. Ways should be found to keep the center in close touch with the social work profession, its practice and schools.[19]

---

[19] See Margaret Mead, *Continuities in Cultural Evolution* (New Haven: Yale University Press, 1964), chaps. 14, 15, and 16. At an appropriate time in the development of the social work profession, regular conferences similar to the Gordon Research Conferences in science and a scholarly quarterly journal might be developed in connection with an advanced center. See W. George Parks, "Gordon Research Conferences: Program for 1964," *Science*, Vol. 143, No. 3611 (March 13, 1964), pp. 1203–1205.

This discussion also assumes that social work can and should develop its own theory regarding the psychosocial phenomena with which it is concerned and ways of dealing with them. The concept of social functioning suggested here (consisting of the interaction of two social variables—the coping efforts of people and the demands of their environment) lends itself to generalization. With greater refinement of the concepts and the formulation of hypotheses, it should be possible to identify patterns of interaction between the variables and thus eventually arrive at prediction. This theory will reflect social work's specific orientation and will be at the center of its knowledge. Other theory from a variety of sources is needed but cannot be effectively put to work in practice until social work develops a sufficiently clear focus and frame of reference so that such relevant knowledge can be incorporated within it.

As pointed out in the preceding chapter, knowledge and value are a source of power for social work in two ways. When a common body of knowledge can be used by all social workers, the scope of their practice will expand. It will probably be found that some theory is soundly used only within the context of certain human relationships, for instance, when a social worker is working with an emotionally disturbed client. But much knowledge and theory will now have broader application than before. When knowledge and theory were tied to separate methods and blended with skill, the schools of social work had to teach the three methods to convey the knowledge. Now the process can be reversed and the knowledge can be taught in its own right, thus becoming available for all practitioners to use in many interventive approaches and operations.

In their anxiety over human needs and rights, social workers have at times been overambitious in their goals and efforts. A single profession cannot be expected to solve basic problems of destitution or service delivery to a total population. Inability to meet such enormous problems should not be regarded as failure by either social workers or others. Social workers should and can, however, set their goals more broadly than they did in the past. The "retreat to the technician" and "overprofessionalism" developed in social work practice before the movement toward a common base and were due to the fact that the base did not exist.

The new trend toward convergence in thinking and increased consensus is beginning to counteract the divisive forces that operated for so long and can lead to integration. This is not the time to lose confidence in the profession for its past deficiencies when it is now moving toward their correction.

Once actually in the process of formation, a professional perspective develops its own force and momentum. Pressure from society and the existence of obviously unmet needs accelerate the process. Each element sets up requirements for, enters into, and draws from the others. Practice experience generates new concepts about helping services, while advancing knowledge stimulates experiments in new interventive approaches. The dysjunction in social work thinking between concentration on the skilled practitioner (the method-and-skill approach) and recognition of the full scope of the profession's practice (the professional approach) could obstruct final movement toward a common base. A major concern of this monograph is how these two phases of social work thinking, each with its own validity and potential, can and should be brought together. Ultimately, all such problems are solved in one way or another in every profession or the profession dies or is transformed. The struggle between knowing and doing, between depth and breadth, runs throughout social work. Meanwhile, recognition of the common base is growing, with just enough force and consistency to permit the profession to hold onto and develop its own strengths.

If we take the early social work characteristics of a strong commitment to help people and to improve their conditions, combined with sensitivity and professional discipline, we have a good beginning for a professional base. If we now add clearly established bodies of value and knowledge, developed and used together, we have greatly enlarged the profession's potential. In our scientifically oriented society, a profession must rest its practice on knowledge in order to influence planning and have an impact on change. Pure knowledge in the form of science and the technology resulting from it have forced radical changes in our society. This is a problem to which many scientists have given serious thought. It appears, however, that knowledge can be a power for good if it is used consciously and planfully to enhance human potential.

We live in one of the great transitional periods of human civilization. As societal problems mount, experts are turning their
attention to the future. Man has "created a world," says Hauser,
"in which mankind itself is the crucial environment—a mankind
characterized by large numbers, high densities, and great hetero-
geneity. He is still learning how to live in this world he has
created." [20] Writers and thinkers are pointing out that in such a
heavily populated world, in spite of a democratic concern for
individual freedom, societal regulation will necessarily increase,
just to make it possible for so many people to live together in
an orderly way. There will be a greater need for experts to work
in teams because of the complexity of problems. There will be
greater need to value the individual, to help people feel that
they are a part of society through increased participation.[21] Today's youth movement, while critical of and often hostile to society,
contains many articulate young people who insist that all people
must be involved in a meaningful way in the decisions that shape
their lives.[22] One is struck by the fact that for some time social
workers have been trying to work in the very directions indicated
as important for the future, such as understanding the meaning
of situations to the people involved, increasing their participation,
and viewing social problems as interrelated. Thus a profession
like social work, which is not authoritarian and identifies with
people who are coping with life problems, is timely and relevant
and will be even more so in the future.

At this point we are reminded of Julian Huxley's answer to
the question, "What are people for?" quoted on the opening page
of this monograph. "To achieve a higher quality of life," he
replied. One of the great advances of our century has been man's
increased understanding of himself. In their eagerness to effect
change in social services and social institutions, it is to be hoped
that social workers will not be pulled away from their primary

---

[20] Philip M. Hauser, "The Chaotic Society: Product of the Social
Morphological Revolution," *American Sociological Review,* Vol. 34, No. 1
(February 1969), pp. 1–19.

[21] "Toward the Year 2000: Work in Progress," *Daedalus,* Vol. 96, No. 3
(Summer 1967), whole issue.

[22] "Symposium on Confrontation: The Old Left and the New," *American Scholar,* Vol. 36, No. 4 (Autumn 1967), pp. 567–588.

orientation to people. In the past, one of social work's major efforts was directed toward helping the individual understand himself and his problems. Could this effort now be expanded to help people in their groups and communities to understand themselves—their limitations, complexities, and potential as human beings—so that they can play an increasingly responsible part in moving toward a higher quality of life for all?

It may be that in using value and knowledge together in the way they do, in focusing on the relation between people's coping efforts and the demands of the environment and in assuming a stance of identification and involvement with the people who have the problems, social workers will be moving toward a social invention—a genuinely creative approach to helping that is adapted to today's society. Social workers have not always held to this approach but have demonstrated that it can be done. The trends are in this direction. The evidence is mounting that our society needs a profession like social work with its particular focus and orientation, and that no other profession is on the way to make this contribution. This beginning might even develop into a kind of service not yet perceived or offered in Western civilization. What social work is trying to do is difficult and has been approached on an uneven course. Yet we seem to be arriving at something not discovered or tried by any other occupational group in the same way, so that our growing perspective is likely to prove distinctive. Social work may not succeed, but it is a splendid quest and worthy of all our effort.

appendix

working definition of
social work practice

(*Reprinted from* SOCIAL WORK, *Vol. 3, No. 2, April 1958.*)

Social work practice, like the practice of all professions, is recognized by a constellation of value, purpose, sanction, knowledge, and method. No part alone is characteristic of social work practice nor is any part described here unique to social work. It is the particular content and configuration of this constellation which makes it social work practice and distinguishes it from the practice of other professions. The following is an attempt to spell out the components of this constellation in such a way as to include all social work practice with all its specializations. This implies that some social work practice will show a more extensive use of one or the other of the components but it is social work practice only when they are all present to some degree.

Value

Certain philosophical concepts are basic to the practice of social work, namely:
1. The individual is the primary concern of this society.
2. There is interdependence between individuals in this society.
3. They have social responsibility for one another.
4. There are human needs common to each person, yet each person is essentially unique and different from others.
5. An essential attribute of a democratic society is the realization of the full potential of each individual and the assumption of his social responsibility through active participation in society.
6. Society has a responsibility to provide ways in which obstacles to this self-realization (*i.e.*, disequilibrium between the individual and his environment) can be overcome or prevented.

These concepts provide the philosophical foundation for social work practice.

Purpose

The practice of social work has as its purposes:

1. To assist individuals and groups to identify and resolve or minimize problems arising out of disequilibrium between themselves and their environment.

2. To identify potential areas of disequilibrium between individuals or groups and the environment in order to prevent the occurrence of disequilibrium.

3. In addition to these curative and preventive aims, to seek out, identify, and strengthen the maximum potential in individuals, groups, and communities.

Sanction *(i.e., authoritative permission; countenance, approbation, or support)*

Social work has developed out of a community recognition of the need to provide services to meet basic needs, services which require the intervention of practitioners trained to understand the services, themselves, the individuals, and the means for bringing all together. Social work is not practiced in a vacuum or at the choice of its practitioners alone.   Thus, there is a social responsibility inherent in the practitioner's role for the way in which services are rendered.   The authority and power of the practitioner and what he represents to the clients and group members derive from one or a combination of three sources:

1. *Governmental agencies* or their subdivisions (authorized by law).

2. *Voluntary incorporated agencies,* which have taken responsibility for meeting certain of the needs or providing certain of the services necessary for individual and group welfare.

3. *The organized profession,* which in turn can sanction individuals for the practice of social work and set forth the educational and other requirements for practice and the conditions under which that practice may be undertaken, whether or not carried out under organizational auspices.

Knowledge

Social work, like all other professions, derives knowledge from a variety of sources and in application brings forth further knowledge from its own processes.   Since knowledge of man is never final or absolute, the social worker in his application of this knowledge takes into account those phenomena that are exceptions to existing generalizations and is aware and ready to deal with the spontaneous and unpredictable in human behavior.   The practice of the social worker is typically guided by knowledge of:

1. Human development and behavior characterized by emphasis on the wholeness of the individual and the reciprocal influences of man and his total environment—human, social, economic, and cultural.

2. The psychology of giving and taking help from another person or source outside the individual.

3. Ways in which people communicate with one another and give outer expression to inner feelings, such as words, gestures, and activities.

4. Group process and the effects of groups upon individuals and the reciprocal influence of the individual upon the group.

5. The meaning and effect on the individual, groups, and community of cultural heritage including its religious beliefs, spiritual values, law, and other social institutions.

6. Relationships, *i.e.*, the interactional processes between individuals, between individual and groups, and between group and group.

7. The community, its internal processes, modes of development and change, its social services and resources.

8. The social services, their structure, organization, and methods.

9. Himself, which enables the individual practitioner to be aware of and to take responsibility for his own emotions and attitudes as they affect his professional functions.

Method (*i.e., an orderly systematic mode of procedure. As used here, the term encompasses social casework, social group work, and community organization*)

The social work method is the responsible, conscious, disciplined use of self in a relationship with an individual or group. Through this relationship the practitioner facilitates interaction between the individual and his social environment with a continuing awareness of the reciprocal effects of one upon the other. It facilitates change: (1) within the individual in relation to his social environment; (2) of the social environment in its effect upon the individual; (3) of both the individual and the social environment in their interaction.

Social work method includes systematic observation and assessment of the individual or group in a situation and the formulation of an appropriate plan of action. Implicit in this is a continuing evaluation regarding the nature of the relationship between worker and client or group, and its effect on both the participant individual or group and on the worker himself. This evaluation provides the basis for the professional judgment which the worker must constantly make and which determines the direction of his activities. The method is used predominantly in interviews, group sessions, and conferences.

Techniques (*i.e., instrument or tool used as a part of method*). Incorporated in the use of the social work method may be one or more of the following techniques in different combinations: (1) support, (2) clarification, (3) information-giving, (4) interpretation, (5) development of insight, (6) differentiation of the social worker from the indi-

vidual or group, (7) identification with agency function, (8) creation
and use of structure, (9) use of activities and projects, (10) provision
of positive experiences, (11) teaching, (12) stimulation of group interaction, (13) limit-setting, (14) utilization of available social resources,
(15) effecting change in immediate environmental forces operating upon
the individual or groups, (16) synthesis.

Skill (*i.e.*, technical expertness; the ability to use knowledge effectively and readily in execution or performance). Competence in social
work practice lies in developing skill in the use of the method and its
techniques described above. This means the ability to help a particular
client or group in such a way that they clearly understand the social
worker's intention and role, and are able to participate in the process
of solving their problems. Setting the stage, the strict observance of
confidentiality, encouragement, stimulation or participation, empathy,
and objectivity are means of facilitating communication. The individual social worker always makes his own creative contribution in
the application of social work method to any setting or activity.

As a way of increasing skill and providing controls to the activity
of the social work practitioner, the following are utilized: (1) recording, (2) supervision, (3) case conferences, (4) consultation, (5) review
and evaluation.

Teaching, Research, Administration

Three important segments of social work, namely, teaching, research,
and administration, have significance for the development, extension,
and transmission of knowledge of social work practice. These have
many elements in common with social work practice, but in addition
have their own uniqueness and some different objectives.

3/70—3.5M—P&K
3/71—3M